The Skeleton Code

The Skeleton Code

A Satirical Guide to Secret Keeping

Alla Campanella

Ken Massey

New York

The Skeleton Code

A Satirical Guide to Secret Keeping

Published in New York, New York, by Morgan James Publishing. Morgan James and The Entrepreneurial Publisher are trademarks of Morgan James, LLC. www.MorganJamesPublishing.com

The Morgan James Speakers Group can bring authors to your live event. For more information or to book an event visit The Morgan James Speakers Group at www.TheMorganJamesSpeakersGroup.com.

ISBN 978-1-63047-953-4 paperback
ISBN 978-1-63047-954-1 eBook
ISBN 978-1-63047-955-8 hardcover
Library of Congress Control Number:
2016900928

Shelfie

A **free** eBook edition is available with the purchase of this print book.

CLEARLY PRINT YOUR NAME ABOVE IN UPPER CASE

Instructions to claim your free eBook edition:
1. Download the Shelfie app for Android or iOS
2. Write your name in **UPPER CASE** above
3. Use the Shelfie app to submit a photo
4. Download your eBook to any device

Cover Design by:
Alex Snart

Interior Design by:
Bonnie Bushman
The Whole Caboodle Graphic Design

Morgan James
The Entrepreneurial Publisher™

Builds

with...

Habitat for Humanity®
Peninsula and
Greater Williamsburg

In an effort to support local communities, raise awareness and funds, Morgan James Publishing donates a percentage of all book sales for the life of each book to

Habitat for Humanity Peninsula and Greater Williamsburg.
Get involved today! Visit
www.MorganJamesBuilds.com

Table of Contents

Preface

Skeletons...

They don't just come out for Halloween. Most of the time, they stay hidden and impatient in our closets. Skeletons are secrets from the past or present that haunt a person's happiness. Some are minor but embarrassing indiscretions perfect for coffee room gossip or neighborhood jokes. Other skeletons, however, would make a priest choke during confession.

Some closeted skeletons sit quietly behind old coats and stacked boxes. Others scratch and rattle doors, trying to slip out of their cells at all hours of the day or night. They play a perpetual game of hide and seek, but are clearly more interested in being found.

Skeletons have their own agenda, and they are largely misunderstood. When their owners want them to be quiet, they aren't. When their landlords want them to disappear, they come out to play. When people try to forget about them, they find new ways to show up. They are uncooperative and unpredictable. This is both good and bad news.

The Good News

Skeletons are truly fun to discover and play with…when they belong to someone else. They are like an extra 20 pounds: You hate your own, but it's kind of fun to see them show up on your frenemy or snooty co-worker. Is there anything more delectable than a skeleton that slips out of the right person's closet? How about the person who stole your boyfriend? Wouldn't you love to know a secret about the person who reported you to the boss? Our personal favorite is catching sight of a skeleton in the closet of that morally superior prude (they always have the best skeletons by far). Discovering these skeletons is like Christmas morning when you were a kid.

There is no question—other people's secrets have long captured our imaginations and fueled our amusements. Where would gossip be if not for great secrets? How can you beat finding out that Ms. Perfect spent the night in jail for drunk and disorderly? What's better than hearing Mr. Macho faints at the sight of blood?

This book is full of skeletons—real ones: the kinds that have haunted people for years. What you won't find here are those that represent real tragedy: injury, abuse, or criminal offense toward others. There is no amusement in fugitive skeletons.

The secrets we are going to share will make you laugh and cringe. They are closeted confidences that represent thoughts, feelings, and actions that, if discovered, would be very embarrassing or problematic to relationships or reputations. Some of these skeletons are cultural or social taboos, and others are personal idiosyncrasies from which others might recoil or decide to renegotiate a relationship. In other words, we are going to tell you the secrets common to humankind; the ones that you would find in every friend's closet if they let you look.

The Bad News

This book is more than reality literature, however. We are not exposing skeletons for the simple pleasure involved. We are also fascinated and frustrated by the ways people try to keep their skeletons safe. A few are successful, but most closet keepers don't have a clue!

So here's the bad news: YOUR SECRETS ARE NOT SECURE!

The REAL reason we wrote this book is so that YOUR skeletons don't end up doing the striptease on social media, or choking your grandma when she hears about them during Thanksgiving dinner. With cameras and recorders on every phone, there are a million opportunities for your skeletons to be discovered.

Please believe us. You won't be able to enjoy hearing someone else's secrets if you're not protecting your own. Make sure you stay on the laughing end of this arrangement because the weeping end is no fun at all. We have written this book to help you become an expert at closet security.

Do you realize how much money people spend to protect their identity from theft? We also pay to protect our homes, our financial assets, our bodies, and our lives. But guess what stays unprotected? The secret that could turn the rest of your life upside down! What are you thinking?

You need to take positive and practical steps to protect your good name. Haven't you worked hard to shape your reputation? It could be gone with one slip of the tongue. It could crash with one errant text or post. If you care about your public presence at all, take steps to protect your persona. That's what *The Skeleton Code* is about. Other books tell you how to keep your body healthy, and we tell you how to keep your closet shut.

Imagine your skeletons are in a federal witness protection program. They are given new identities and taken far away from those who might like to find them. *The Skeleton Code* contains proven methods to move your skeletons to a place where they can't be found by friend or foe. You simply can't be sloppy with secrets or they will find a way out.

You might also think of your secrets as inmates who need maximum security complete with razor wire, electric fences, observation towers, armed guards, and trained dogs. Our book will give you the equivalent of these safety measures.

How did we get this expertise? We learned it from the masters and perfected it in our own lives. We have secrets (of the non-criminal variety) no one will ever find. Instead of being objects of suspicion or scandal, we are trusted confidants. How do you think we heard all these secrets we are about to share? We have worked with people who decided they could tell us very personal details about their lives. How great is that? We get to hear juicy stories while our skeletons are tucked away in Fort Knox. Of course, we have changed names and details to protect the identity of our friends and family who have given us a peek at their closets.

If you follow *The Skeleton Code*, you will stay off the gossip grapevine at work or in the family. If you practice the principles we suggest, your closet will be more secure than your portfolio, and you can be the laugh-er instead of the laugh-ee.

Should you, against our advice, ever decide to come out of your closet, and again, we strongly urge you to maintain appearances, then we also conclude this book with some advice about coming clean. We do recognize that some people say they enjoy life more when they are transparent, but we don't believe it. Yet because we are equal opportunity advice givers, we thought we should include something for those who think it's important to be real.

We hope you enjoy comparing your skeletons to those in this book. No matter what you have in your closet, you'll find something interesting in this one. Enjoy!

Additional Guidelines For Reading *The Skeleton Code*

For those readers who may not appreciate the subtleties of satire, we offer this advice:

- Do not follow any expressed or implied methods in this book to commit illegal acts;
- Do not use the ideas in this book to engage in covert behavior against any government;
- Do not practice any of the techniques in this book to the detriment of other persons;
- Do not use the skills in this book to become a successful politician;
- Do not hide this book in your closet;
- Do not operate heavy machinery while reading this book;
- Do not use this book to start fires, literally or figuratively;
- Do not use this book as a traditional or alternative medicine;
- Do not start a religion with this book (a fan club would be OK);
- Do not try to figure out the true identity of the people we talk about in this book;
- Do not use this book as a weapon, a pillow, or a flotation device.

Acknowledgements

We should probably thank our parents, other family members and friends, but then this would read like an Academy Award speech, so we'll keep it short.

This book was inspired by the openness and vulnerability of friends, family and colleagues we have known along the way. Our lives have been shaped by so many and we are grateful for their insights and for their stories.

We want to thank everyone on our publishing team at Morgan James. You guys were consummate professionals as you guided us on this amazing journey.

Justin Spizman did our major editing and he was skilled and relentless, which is what we needed. We so appreciate his contributions.

We loved the cover concept in our heads but needed someone who could make it a reality. Thank you Morgan James for getting us started, and Alex Snart for putting it all together with wizardry and artistry. We love what you created!

Lastly, we would like to thank each other for this labor of love. It was a long, difficult and collaborative effort that stretched our gifts and drew on the diversity of our experiences. We are pleased to share the final product with you.

Introduction

Even a small leak can sink a great ship.
—**Benjamin Franklin**

Everyone is feeling insecure these days. The market is volatile. Computers are exposed to hackers. Our political system is shaky. Global conflict is becoming a malignancy. And worst of all, you have skeletons in a closet with no security system! It's time to *put your secrets in the closet, lock the door, and throw away the key.*

Why do you need to care about this kind of personal security? Perhaps this story will explain:

One Monday morning, three clergymen were enjoying some downtime while fishing on the lake. They were all three grumbling about church matters, as was their Sunday reflection custom.

When the conversation waned, Father Mark said, "You know, I have something weighing on me and don't really have anyone else I can share it with other than you guys. But I'm only going to confess this if each of you shares one of your dark secrets too."

The other two agreed, so Father Mark began.

"I've been helping myself to some of the offering each Sunday," he said, looking more playful than convicted.

"How much?," one of the others asked.

"I don't know. Just a few hundred dollars."

"Total?"

"No, each week."

"A few hundred each week!? How long have you been doing this?"

"Well I've been at St. Mary's a dozen years, so I guess it's been that long. If they paid me what I was worth, I wouldn't have to take any tips. I can't imagine how I'd make ends meet otherwise. So, that's my dark secret. What about you guys?"

Jim was next. He led the prominent Presbyterian congregation in town.

"I have a weakness about the truth," he said sheepishly.

"What do you mean by that?" asked Father Mark.

"I mean I kind of cut corners with it."

"How big are the corners?"

"Look I'm a pathological liar, OK!!! I just can't help myself. Half my resume is fiction. The stories I tell and the names I drop are made up on the spot. Lying has always been my way of getting out of tight spots and impressing people. I get my sermons on the Internet, for God's sake! If the church knew this, they would toss me out on my ear."

The other ministers sat there dumbfounded for a moment.

Then Jim said, "How about you, Ed? Surely the Baptist minister has a weakness too."

"Oh yes," said Ed in his southern drawl, "I have lots of 'em. But I suppose my biggest weakness is that I'm an incurable gossip! Never kept a secret in my life."

The Skeleton Problem

We know you are offended *and* delighted when you get a glimpse of skeletons in other people's closets. And most of the time, you can't wait to pass it along! Everyone loves a juicy tale more than the boring truth. "Oh the moral outrage of what people do these days…I can't wait to text Liz about it!"

The higher these fallen friends and heroes are on the food chain, the better. That's why we have tabloids, TMZ, and Entertainment Tonight. Scandalous! Delicious! Can you believe that Miley Cyrus affair? Have you seen the UFO picture that was smuggled out of Area 51? As it turns out, Dick Cheney really is a robot.

Scandals that come to light are like hurricanes, however. They're only interesting if they're crashing someone else's coast. Let's face it, we don't really believe in the right to privacy. We believe in the right to OUR privacy. The rest is fair game for our amusement.

So to make sure your scandals don't come home to roost, or find their way into social media sensations, we have developed a guide that will keep your skeletons safe behind lock and key. With our principles, called The Skeleton Code, you can live a life of pristine pretense.

As one song by Elizabeth and the Catapult suggests:

But once the lights come up,
It will be like it never happened;
And is that really such a bad thing?

"Like it never happened." That's our goal for you. You can learn to keep your secrets safe and secure. It doesn't matter if your skeletons are long retired and collecting dust, or are as fresh as last night's impropriety, we can help make sure your secrets don't find their way onto the cover of "National Enquirer," or onto the lips of your neighborhood gossip.

In so doing, we will help you maintain your good name and your status in the community...all without hiring an expensive personal image consultant. Not only can our book save you thousands of dollars in professional fees, our plan will insure that you avoid devastating embarrassments that can wreak havoc on your reputation.

We have spent years doing research on skeleton maintenance and have distilled our knowledge into clear and compelling strategies. For the very first time anywhere, you will read the wisdom of the world's greatest secret-keepers. You will see how real people failed to follow these principles and suffered the consequences.

There are two kinds of people in the world: those with skeletons running rampant and those with skeletons safely tucked away. The former is a disaster waiting to happen, and this book will make sure yours stay put.

In these pages, you will learn the strategies that have protected politicians and socialites alike. You will be able to use this guide to develop your own Personal Pretense Plan, guaranteed to secure whatever is rattling around in your closet.

Chapter One

Dress For Diversion

Dressing well can open all doors.
—Adapted from **Thomas Fuller**

D ressing well may open some doors, but it can also close a very important one: the one to your skeleton closet! We agree with Euripides, who 2,500 years ago said, "Know first who you are and then adorn yourself accordingly." We say, know first how you want to be perceived and what you're hiding, and then create a persona to emphasize the former and cover the latter. Who better to dress to impress than those with counter-impressive secrets to hide?

In this chapter, we will address two Skeleton Code approaches to dressing for diversion. First, you will need to create a general and overarching identity as a fine upstanding citizen of unquestioned character. Don't worry, it's not as difficult as it sounds.

Second, you will need to craft a more specific alter ego based on the unique skeletons you are hiding in your closet. If you're hiding racism, for instance, you may want to join the NAACP or maybe just get one of their bumper stickers. We call this technique Accentuate the Positive. Let's look first at the big picture...

The Big Persona

We all judge books (and people) by their covers. Thank God we can create a good cover. Anyone can manage appearances. Your mission, and it's not impossible, is to cover up well, to dress the part, and to perfect the pretense. Attractive works, but only if it attracts people away from your secrets. You can learn to give your audience visual clues that give a Mother Teresa affect, even if you have Paris Hilton DNA.

Seldom do people discern deception behind an expensive dress, classy suit, or fine array of the right accessories. And yes, we are speaking literally and metaphorically. The "Shallow Hal" world is not limited to Hollywood. Ours is a skin-deep culture from east to west, enamored with outward appearance and surface judgment, unless there is a compelling reason to go deeper.

A careless scandal would be one of those reasons. Don't give your audience any cause to be curious about what's beneath your polished exterior. We don't have to go deep with your persona, but we do have to be thoughtful and thorough.

We need to move beyond the limited help of a publicity agent or image consultant. These professionals may help you present yourself in a way that is most advantageous to your professional career, but they have ethical limitations that make them ineffective for skeleton work. Modifying a resume to keep a skeleton at bay would be a case in point.

In the professional world, some curious prospective employer could pry into your reality. They could get access to official documents like transcripts, birth certificates, and criminal background information. For closet concealment, you'll need more than any marketing make-up artist can provide.

When it comes to your personal image, think big. You need to stretch your façade from horizon to horizon. You are not limited to the present or to recent history in this effort. Clear and consistent stories from childhood are powerful shapers of image, especially if they are stories of overcoming tragedy. Be careful to avoid too much drama. Some people will try to uncover old news stories if the episode is too fantastic.

> When it comes to your personal image, think big. You need to stretch your façade from horizon to horizon.

Your visible and verbal image is your first and most important line of defense against closet invasion. The more grounded you seem on the surface, the less curiosity or concern you will create. The more "padding" you can use in the creation of your character, the better—especially when there are significant risks rattling around in your closet.

Certain liberties in massaging your image are not only acceptable; they are also absolutely necessary. You can also be certain that your friends are doing the same. They are dropping names of people they've never met. They are telling about how they stopped to give aid at the scene of an accident when all they really did was slow down to gawk.

You can develop better skills than these and rise above their clumsy and ill-fated efforts.

Too Close For Comfort

The greatest challenge to big persona success is a too close relationship like marriage or deep friendship. It's really hard to have secure closets in close quarters. If you have large skeletons and an impressive image to protect, you might want to stay away from both of these, or at least recognize the long-term challenges and risks. They can be overcome, but not without real finesse, such as we found with this couple.

Matt and Tiffany learned to dress for diversion because of a marital skeleton. They met and fell in love during college. Matt was from New York and Tiffany was from South Carolina, but they found each other 'different' in the most intriguing ways.

Matt was an outgoing and confident young man—a real straight-talker. Tiffany thought his honesty and openness was a refreshing change from the young southern men she had known. Tiffany was intelligent and refined, but soft-spoken and tenderhearted, which made Matt feel a warmth and connection he had never known with anyone in New York.

Their relationship quickly became passionate and exclusive, and the two became inseparable. The warm emotions of the relationship came in waves…over and over again. They felt completely alive and in love.

Five years later, Tiffany was wishing Matt would die—a rather striking skeleton in her closet. She was taking Prozac and Trazadone for her depression. Matt actually had an appointment at the World Trade Center on 9/11 that was cancelled at the last minute and Tiffany kept fantasizing, "if only he had been up there in that office." She was miserable and couldn't tell a soul.

Divorce wasn't an option in her family, nor did it seem like a secure move for her future. She had put her career on hold so that Matt could get established in the financial world. If she divorced, she would have only settlement money and no job. She didn't know how she would survive or where she would go. It would be so much better if he would die in an accident. She would have the insurance money and an outpouring of support rather than judgment about a failed marriage.

What she didn't know was that Matt had the same feelings about her. He was sick of her Southern passive aggressiveness. He had no real qualms about divorce, only financial fears about the settlement. Of course, he would never do anything to actually hurt his wife. He just wanted her to go away—permanently and inexpensively.

His and hers closets with matching skeletons are more common than you can imagine. And what a great challenge and frequent necessity to keep important secrets from those you live with! Matt and Tiffany did this well because desperation really is the mother of invention. They knew the personas they had developed to be successful in life were not sufficient to secure their new secrets. They needed big personas because they were hiding their skeletons from someone living in the same house.

Tiffany masked her marital displeasure in public like a true Southerner. She always adorned herself with a smile when others were around. She pursued every possible outing with friends, which accomplished two purposes. First, she could actually enjoy some company and laughter, neither of which she experienced at home. And second, in these settings where mingling was expected, she could stay disconnected from Matt in a way that did not raise suspicions.

Matt was less creative. He simply spent more time at work, but made sure he kept pictures of his wife in prominent places on his desk, and spoke "lovingly" to her when they were in public. It was a typically male strategy with short-term prospects for success. Matt kept collecting more skeletons in his closet and eventually they went on parade, followed by a divorce and expensive settlement.

We are not surprised. Not many understand the challenges of closet maintenance in up-close situations. Had Matt had access to the insights in this book, he could have made his image bulletproof.

To protect the skeletons of marital discord, we suggest that you:

- Happily attend large group events together during which you can evade time with your partner/spouse.
- Share stories about what your spouse is doing, especially when those stories show them in a positive light.
- Avoid public disagreements, which usually means keeping your distance in public.
- Do not exceed your closet's maximum capacity. A closet can quickly reach a tipping point.
- Many marital skeletons require closet agreements (I won't look in yours if you won't look in mine).

The Power of Trajectory

There are many ways to dress for diversion or deception in order to keep your skeletons tucked away. If you promise not to become complacent, a cardinal violation of the Code, we will tell you some good news. Use it to your advantage, but don't make it your only strategy.

Here's the perk. If you make a good first impression, it goes a long, long way! Most people tend to trust their initial assessments of others. Once you've taken a trustworthy trajectory in someone's mind, it's difficult to alter that course. Assumption work is alive and well in our world and it's almost priceless.

The power of trajectory is a huge advantage when maintaining an image. It's like mass and momentum. The more gravitas you give to your persona, the harder it becomes for anything to alter its course. When the arc of your identity is moving in one direction, it tends to keep moving in that direction.

This is why you need to launch your personality in the opposite direction from your secret. What that means, in the vast majority of cases, is that you don't have to overwhelm people with your virtue or character. You don't have to dress to the 10's all the time like they do on Downton Abbey. Simply exude confidence in your persona, stay on course, and avoid any serious wardrobe or closet malfunctions. Most people will assume you are who you present yourself to be. Like we said, it's not as difficult as it seems.

The Second Nature Principle

You may be wondering how you can constantly maintain your persona, even with the power of positive trajectory. We understand the concern, so here's more good news that we call the Second Nature Principle. The more you dress for diversion, the more you'll feel the part. It's a psychological dynamic familiar to every actor who gets more and more into a character. Walter found this truth accidentally.

Walter, an older gentleman, would no longer attend his Baptist church because he didn't have a good suit to wear. This word came to the attention of the church deacons who took a collection to buy the man a new suit. It was the nicest suit he had ever owned.

The next Sunday morning came along and Walter never showed up at his church. With a bit of alarm, two deacons went to his house to check on him. They rang the doorbell and soon he appeared, still wearing his new suit.

The visitors were confused and said, "We missed you this morning and wanted to make sure you were OK."

"I'm fine," Walter said with a smile. "I got up this morning and put on my new suit, looked at myself in the mirror and thought, 'you know, you look good enough to go to the Episcopal Church.'"

The great thing about dressing for diversion is that it not only works on others, but after a while it also starts to work on you. You begin to

The great thing about dressing for diversion is that it not only works on others, but after a while it also starts to work on you.

believe the ideal you is the real you. Use the Second Nature Principle, live into your character, and soon it will fit like a glove, and we don't mean O.J.'s.

Let's pause and take a moment to review where we've been. To achieve closet security, we need first to have a nice cover, like the cover of our book. We need to attempt good first impressions, regardless of how shallow. We need to be clear about the challenges that close relationships present, and we can celebrate the tendencies that make all of this easier for us: the power of momentum and our ability to live into our upstanding persona.

Two crucial strategies that will support these efforts are:

1. Key Public Relationships

We all do guilt and innocence by association. Make sure you are seen with those who are known to be upstanding citizens. It's that "birds of a feather" thing and it works. Get to know influential neighbors. Volunteering can put you in proximity to image icons.

This principle also applies to organizations. An excellent way to create a general impression about your integrity is to participate in a religious community. Make sure this community has bumper stickers or other identification you can place on your car. What good is being associated with religion if no one knows? Remember to stay away from fundamentalist churches. Those people will try to get into your business. Find a larger church that won't notice whether you attend or not.

One can also drop churchy language into conversation as a way of creating a preferred personality. Stay away from religious controversy and limit your comments to themes such as tolerance, respect, and helping the poor. You may think this is difficult if you are not already associated with a religion, but as the truism suggests: Appearing to be religious is easy, even if being religious is not.

Most churches have activities designed for outsiders like picnics, festivals and concerts. These are great low-intimidation places to start. Try to meet a clergy person and remember their name for use. If there are other public figures present, introduce yourself. Most will not put pressure on you to engage in church life unless you act really interested.

If you feel guilty or get bad vibes in a religious setting, don't give up. Instead, volunteer with a prominent non-profit in your community. If you take the diet approach, it won't take that much time. One does not actually have to work on a Habitat house to fly their colors. A small donation will let you mention your support. One might also find a non-profit T-shirt or mug at Goodwill. Just browse their store and you'll find all types of non-profit giveaway items that you can place in your workspace or wear to the gym.

We have found that the best way to solidify your image as a true volunteer is to advocate for a non-profit by taking up a collection. This puts you in direct contact with the people you need to impress at work or in your neighborhood, wherever the cover is most needed. If you do collect money, or goods, we recommend actually giving the collection to the non-profit! Otherwise, you'll have another rather difficult skeleton to keep. Just visit their websites. Most will outline how you can help.

In trying to create a general impression of good citizenship, we aren't as keen on joining clubs like Rotary or Kiwanis because they actually expect you to go to weekly meetings. Who has time for that, especially when there are so many less-demanding alternatives? We feel that religious groups are better because they have millions of members who never participate.

Remember, the key to this strategy is visibility. If people can't see your connection to respectability and learn to appreciate your association, what's the point?

2. Keep It Mono-Polar

Consistency is the gold standard for every public image strategy. Whatever rhythm of character you choose, maintain a steady beat. Pace yourself. Stay in your lane. Use cruise control. Your life cannot resemble Ping-Pong balls in a tile bathroom. An erratic persona sets off alarms. Stability is the code that turns them off.

What do we mean? Mood swings, for instance, are a liability. We know there are often chemical or genetic reasons for these fluctuations, so use pharmaceuticals if there's any question (better life through drugs). There are many good mood stabilizers on the market. Some are legal. If you can't get a prescription, you'll have to keep yourself steady using more rudimentary techniques like counting to 100 or putting yourself in timeout.

The point is, when you're a Pollyanna one moment and a poltergeist the next, it raises suspicions about just how close or over the edge you might live! The Dr. Jekyll and Mr. Hyde game will draw unnecessary attention to yourself. You do not want questions or curiosity swirling around your life when you're protecting skeletons.

There are some exceptions to this rule. Men watching sports are allowed to act out primitive warfare rituals. And women who find out they are dating a cheater have permission to melt down and do that Carrie Underwood *Before He Cheats* stuff. Your big persona can have rises and falls, but it can't bounce around like Twitter stock.

We also encourage you to avoid "splitting," which is a counterproductive defense mechanism that calls too much attention to one's critical personality. We want a good defense to be sure, but not this one. Even if you see the world as "black and white" and naturally think of everyone and everything as either good or bad, resist. It doesn't work! When you demonize and/or idolize others, it raises questions about borderline personality disorder. It also invites others to practice the same exercise on you, which we want to avoid. We want you to be experienced as the consummately balanced person.

We know a younger man named Sam who was having trouble with emotional ups and downs. He would be energetic and hopeful one minute and lethargic and melancholy the next. His first business venture had gone bust. It was a huge blow to his ego, and Sam never wanted to mention it to anyone, including his new wife. It was in the past and he wanted to forget about it, but the pain still haunted him in ways he didn't realize. He needed to dress for diversion and we encouraged him to find a way to do that.

Sam started wearing a Superman T-shirt under his dress shirt when he went to work. It didn't work with white shirts, but that wasn't a big deal. It was his way of saying that the earlier failure was just a fleeting Kryptonite moment. He was going to be a success in life and he wanted to dress the part. Of course, he could not let anyone see this, as it would have led to a psychological evaluation. He actually liked doing something that would sear his new public image into his mind. The shirt gave him courage and confidence when those old thoughts of failure returned. He would simply go to the restroom mirror, unbutton the dress shirt, pull it open in Clark Kent fashion, and *up, up and away*, he felt a surge of confidence and energy.

Sure, the t-shirt was another secret for Sam to manage, but we applaud his super success mentality and his commitment to consistency. If he lives into that new ego as well as he slips into that t-shirt, others will notice and assume that Sam is a successful guy.

We will address other methods and give more examples of creating a general impression of flawless character throughout the book. Now we turn to the second dimension of dressing for diversion, which is devising a particular compensation based upon the unique nature of your skeleton(s).

Accentuate the Positive

John Mitchell, Attorney General of the United States under Richard Nixon, famously asserted, "I am the law and order Attorney General." Shortly thereafter, he was convicted of conspiracy, obstruction of justice, and perjury for his role in the Watergate scandal. Everyone was in disbelief.

We must take note, however, that a very focused strategy of swinging to the opposite end of your closeted character worked for Mr. Mitchell for a long time. He created a larger than life identity as the straight-as-an-arrow, down the middle, no exceptions or excuses law enforcer. He might have gone down in history as one of our great national prosecutors had he not inherited the crazed skeletons that haunted his president.

When you have something rotten in the basement, you need to be generous with the Febreze upstairs. If you're using dandelion greens in your salad, you'll want to go heavy on the sweet dressing. If you have dark bags under your eyes, it's not the time to skimp on the concealer. This is an important theme in *The Skeleton Code*.

You can't simply bury your secret or have some general façade to cover it up. If you want to sell that rundown foreclosure house you picked up, you'll have to do more than throw some paint on it to find a buyer. You'll have to patch the hole in the floor. Those kitchen cabinets with five coats of paint will have to be replaced. So will the moldy shower stall.

It's the same if you're protecting skeletons in your closets. A good reputation is a good start, but you'll need more. You will have to address your specific vulnerabilities by moving your public persona along a continuum to the opposite end of your closeted self. Let us explain.

Imagine a gang member who's been busted on drug and weapons charges. His jeans are full of holes. His jacket has explicit graffiti on it and a small hardware store is pieced through his assorted body parts, seen and unseen. Now flash forward to the hearing where he stands before a judge. The young man is wearing a suit that covers up almost all his ink, and the only metal in his body is a filling in one of his molars. Sure, it's a desperate attempt by his attorney, but it also softens the visual blow for the judge, even though he can see the rap sheet.

This is what you need to be doing *before* you get busted! You must create a persona, or at least a reputational characteristic, that is the virtuous opposite of your scandal. You do this not by ignoring or forgetting your secret, but by using its reversed image to define your public personality. It's important that you keep your new identity on the same continuum as your skeleton. Remember, the purpose is to draw the attention of others away from your secret by moving to the "opposite" pole.

It's not exactly like "hiding in plain sight," but it's close. Take the Dugger family as an over-the-top case in point. It seems that, in addition to being their own version of a population explosion, this family of 21 needed to hide a really bad secret, one outside the law and the purview of this book. They did this in three ways. First, they presented themselves to the outside world as a model family. They extolled their deep and abiding conservative values. That would have been enough, but they went into hyper-drive, deciding to make their family the fodder for a reality television show broadcast around the nation. Instead of looking over their shoulders, they put their collective polished persona on stage for the entire world to see, knowing that the honorable image would divert us from the reality in their closet. It did for a while. Lastly, they became politically active, targeting the very behavior they were hiding in their collective closet.

We don't recommend putting your idealized self on television and making that counter image the focus of a political strategy that could backfire. Simply paint yourself as a person who would never do the thing you actually did. On the continuum of your indiscretion, move to the opposite end and make others take note, within reason. This works for skeleton maintenance like slight of hand works for a magician.

We call it Accentuate the Positive, in honor of Johnny Mercer's old song:

> *You've got to accentuate the positive,*
> *eliminate the negative,*
> *latch on to the affirmative;*
> *don't mess with Mister In-Between.*

No, you cannot actually eliminate the negative, but you can hide it behind a pristine façade by accentuating it's opposite. As the song says, you cannot do this half-way, or "in-between." You really need to amp up the antithesis of what's in your closet if you want to keep your secrets secure.

A Real Cover Girl

Abigail had a gift with computer code and made a great living as owner of a well respected IT security business. Her ventures into hacking started when she was in high school. It was a thrill and she wasn't malicious; just curious about how many firewalls she could get through.

Later, her hacking kept her sharp and better at the security game, yet "breaking and entering" for business just didn't have the same thrill. Hacking into personal computers, especially those of her friends, did make her blood run hotter. The risks were very low, actually, and the payoff was off-the-charts fun. She would find all the secret stuff about her friends and co-workers that wasn't fit for Facebook. She would gain access to pictures that would melt a scrapbook, and she read some titillating commentary that would never be trusted to a diary. Imagine all the skeletons of all your friends on parade and you will get the picture. What a hobby!

Abigail decided early on that she would do this for her own amusement and nothing more. That seemed to work for a while, until she found some unflattering comments about herself and one of her friends. Obviously, she could not confront anyone about what she had seen, but she did find some anonymous ways to get even. It didn't move beyond that until the secret scuffle with Miranda, who was trying to put the move on Abigail's boyfriend.

One day, Miranda received an email from the administrator of MySpace saying that one of the pictures she had posted violated their decency policy and had been removed. She had no idea what picture they were talking about and asked them to send it to her. Sure enough, the photo they sent was Miranda unclothed in bed. An old boyfriend had taken it and she had kept it in her computer but had *never* posted it. She denied the posting vehemently, but the administrator suggested that perhaps she had posted it while under the influence, as often happens.

Once the confusion wore off, she was suddenly mortified about who may have seen it before it was taken down. She spent the next few weeks trying to find out who saw it as she hid away in her apartment. Meanwhile, Abigail was having a lovely time with her boyfriend.

So, how did Abigail practice the antithesis code strategy? How did she publically place herself at the opposite end of the personal security continuum?

First, she would constantly tell her friends and associates how to practice good computer security. She often suggested software and settings that would make their computers more tamper resistant, though she could easily get past these measures when she wanted to surf. *Note: act as a reasonable crusader against your own secret.*

Secondly, she feigned contempt for "those criminals" who broke into people's personal lives and took information for their own benefit. She gleefully told stories of hackers who were headed to prison. Anyone who knew Abigail realized that security was not only her business; it was also her personal passion. *Note: add a visceral quality to your advocacy.*

If any of Abigail's friends ever suspected that their computers had been hacked, two things would happen. First, it would never cross their minds to be suspicious of Abigail. Second, they would immediately reach out to her to help them with the problem! You have to appreciate that irony, and also the strategy called Accentuate the Positive (or opposite).

It's important to remember that you have to be fully committed to this technique. Don't mess with "Mr. In-Between." Halfhearted and sloppy double agents don't survive. You need a good plan, a believable antithesis, and you need to sell it. If you don't, the following could happen...

Another Barney Fife

As reported by most major American news sources, an older man named Robert ran too far with his fantasy. Showing some classic tendencies to over-compensate, he donated money to the local sheriff's election campaign so he could become a reserve sheriff, carry a gun and badge, and play cops and robbers. Unfortunately, he was so focused on the fun parts of his fantasy that he skipped the necessary training, which seems to be possible when you donate enough money. During the excitement of an arrest in April 2015, with a perpetrator on the ground and resisting, he tried to use his Taser to subdue the suspect. Not a bad plan in theory. Sadly, however, the trigger he pulled was not on the stun device but on his 357-magnum pistol. The suspect died.

The reserve officer's story was that he thought he had his Taser in hand. Maybe if he had gone to the required training, instead of being a political contributor, some instructor would have covered the difference between the two pieces of equipment. Now the whole world knows the man was Barney Fife pretending to be Dirty Harry, when he should have kept his bullet in his pocket.

This can happen to you if your positive persona is under-developed or if you approach it half-heartedly. If you're going to pretend to be someone else (and you really need to establish that protective persona if you want to keep your secrets safe), then master the role. You wouldn't read the script once and try to go on stage, so don't settle for a casual compensatory identity either.

A Safe Distance

Remember, there is no perfect swing to the opposite end of your morality spectrum. Cover looks good at a distance, but no make-up job can pass the test of close scrutiny. People who lead double lives often get busted. But it's usually because they were sloppy and distracted or let people get too close. Millions of others enjoy their cover for life. You can be one of those if you work the system.

We read about an Englishman who wanted to tour Europe in his Rolls Royce. He had the car shipped across the channel to France and began his month-long journey. Somewhere in Italy, he developed engine trouble. He called Rolls and they flew a mechanic out to fix his car. That's a perk of which we're not familiar.

When he returned home to England, he called Rolls to express his thanks for the good service. After explaining what had been done to affect the repair, the Rolls Representative said, "I'm very sorry sir, but we have no record of any problems with a Rolls Royce."

Now that's the quality of public reputation we're talking about. When you create that stellar image that is the antithesis of your secret, everyone will know there could never be a problem with your character. Just keep accentuating the positive, and stay away from Mister In-Between.

Tackling Taboos

It should be said that there are some taboos that if broken have greater negative social consequences. For example, wishing you had never had children is a feeling that would be on everyone's "most scandalous thoughts" list. It is almost universally accepted that you should love your children more than yourself, put their interests ahead of your own, and always be immensely grateful for their lives.

Sadie never enjoyed anything about motherhood, starting with hours of labor and a C-section. The work hours of a parent were terrible and there were no discernable benefits other than creating the illusion that time was standing still. She wondered if a husband would have helped, but quickly decided that would only have doubled her trouble. When she heard about that mother from Tennessee who sent her adopted son back to Russia, she wished she had such an option. She wanted to scream this out to someone, but she swallowed it instead.

When her daughter entered adolescence, the battle entered a new stage, one resembling the US campaign in Vietnam. Whenever Sadie made a move, her daughter would retaliate with a new tattoo, piercing, or pregnancy. Sadie didn't have any family, which was just as well. She might have been honest with them about how much she hated being a mother.

When her daughter moved out and halfway across the country, Sadie realized her need for a better way to suppress her pent-up feelings of regret. She had been in conversations when her feelings came much too close to the surface, and if they had, they would have been strong enough to peel paint. When other mothers became sentimental about their children, Sadie could hardly contain herself. She needed a strategy, especially since she was a trusted pediatrician.

To protect her reputation from ruin, Sadie made a public slide to the opposite end of her parenting continuum. Obviously, she could not pretend to be the joyous parent of an estranged daughter, so she decided to craft an image of the loving mother who was supremely injured. By giving her friends and co-workers a close-up view of her daughter's life, she could cushion her regret in the understandable emotion of grief.

In order to brand yourself as a good citizen who is the polar opposite of the skeleton in your closet, consider these effective branding strategies. When you strip it all down, it's basically marketing your image as if it were your finest product.

1. **Achieve and Maintain Clarity About Your Brand.** Write down a clear and compelling definition of the "brand" or persona you are trying to achieve. Post it in a place where you can read it every day.

2. **Create Synergy.** Find ways to integrate various aspects of your life into your personal brand. This includes everything from how you construct your social media image to what emoticons you use in text messages.

3. **Know Your Calling Card.** Use a tagline that expresses your brand and use it in all correspondence. This is your persona "mission statement."

4. **Keep it Consistent:** Really Steady and Stable. Don't present one image in public and a different one on Facebook. Your theme is "That's my story, and I am sticking to it!"

Don't Go Overboard

Can you have too much of a good thing when it comes to a persona? Yes, you can. We strongly advise you to practice perfection with reserve.

We find the story of Miami rapper Rick Ross compelling. He really needed to keep his former profession a secret. You see, Rick, who was born William Roberts II, had been a corrections officer—a career and a reputation that would make life difficult for him if his friends in the hood found out. Rick understood the Code, however, and reinvented himself as a gangsta rapper, a job that made him millions and was more respected in his world. Sadly, news of his past work as a cop came to light. He denied the reports, but the real evidence turned his life upside down.

He pressed his tough image beyond all necessity, living too much into his persona, a real Code violation. He continued to get into trouble with the law, being accused of several violent crimes. Ian Cohen suggested that Ross had become "too good at being fake."

There are limits to how far you can take a persona. When you do this, people will assume you're drinking the same Kool-Aid as Ross and Donald Trump. So we have a pithy saying for you: *You don't need excess to have success!*

So that you will have better luck with your believable persona, we offer you this handy Dress for Diversionary Success Checklist. What should you wear to the party where your secrets might be at risk? How should you present yourself in the meeting where stress could expose your skeletons? If you just imagine dressing for an interview and apply these stylistic principles to your public image, you'll be ready.

Dress For Diversion Checklist

✓ The dark conservative suit of a serious demeanor: To appear completely grounded, balanced, and distinctive from the culture of narcissism and individuality.

✓ The white shirt or blouse of button-downed virtue: To convey the notion of purity with nothing untoward protruding.

✓ The matching belt of holding up appearances: To prevent sagging seemliness or drooping personas.

✓ The clean-shaven look of respectability: To give the smooth appearance of one who maintains the best social standards.

✓ The low-heeled and polished shoes of humility: To avoid the stilettoes of showmanship and the casual look of moral apathy.

✓ The stylish hair of homespun humor: To portray good taste that would never participate in off-color or insensitive humor.

✓ The jewelry and piercing-free appearance of professionalism: To demonstrate social constraint and to convince that pain isn't a favorite pastime.

✓ The tattoo-less image of true tolerance and sensitivity: To demonstrate that you have no need to make glaring social or anti-social statements using your body as a billboard, nor ever wish to make nice older ladies afraid of walking by you on the sidewalk.

✓ The well-manicured nails (without polish) of neatness: To give attention to the small details of your persona as immaculately conceived.

✓ The conventional accessories of civic pride: To show your true colors, try the flag pin of patriotism, the kerchief of fraternity, the handbag of religious devotion, and the cologne of community service.

Chapter Two

Mimic the Masters

"I know how easy it is for one to stay well within moral, ethical, and legal bounds through the skillful use of words—and to thereby spin, sidestep, circumvent, or bend a truth completely out of shape."
—Sidney Poitier

D ressing for diversion is a great way to start your new skeleton code protocol. It is like the first level of firewall protection for your computer system. In this chapter, the next level we cover is also an essential element to your overall security portfolio. We know this because the strategies have been developed by the best secret-keepers on earth. We call them "masters of the craft." You know them as politicians.

Those who excel at any craft have almost always been mentored by at least one exceptional teacher. Often, the difference between good and

22

great is not innate talent, but a connection to great and gifted coaches. Daniel Coyle presents evidence of this pattern in his book, *The Talent Code*, and the paradigm can also be true for those who hide skeletons.

Sadly, most closet custodians are amateurish (before they read our book), bumbling and bungling their secrets. A few, however, rise to greatness because a wise and experienced hand has led them to real security. When it comes to keeping those troublesome secrets, you can't set your sights low. You need to look for the best, love the best, learn from the best, and not worry about the rest.

There's a saying in aviation that "there are old pilots and bold pilots, but there aren't any old bold pilots." Carelessness will crash your future when you take novice chances and make rookie mistakes with your *unspeakables*. Why be reckless with the "explosives" in your closet when there are so many fine veterans of the game who can lead and inspire you to greater security? You want to learn from those who have been successful at keeping a secure closet for years, and who have the status to prove it. Don't just make it up as you go along. Learn from the masters.

What better place to glean these pearls of wisdom than from those who have everything to lose if their skeletons escape? Why not learn from some of the most highly motivated people on the planet? We have closely examined the traits of those who live in a culture of public image and distilled their strategies. Many of these masters have been more adept at skeleton maintenance than their actual profession.

Conveniently, these masters tend to gravitate toward one specific habitat. When it comes to managing a double life, no one is more experienced

When it comes to managing a double life, no one is more experienced and proficient than the politician. Political cover is an evolved and enlightened art form.

and proficient than the politician. Political cover is an evolved and enlightened art form. The depth of expertise found among the political species inspires us.

Mark Twain once said, *Sometimes I wonder whether the world is being run by smart people who are putting us on or by imbeciles who really mean it.* Regarding the work performance of our national leaders, it seems to be the latter, but don't let that fool you. Just because they can't legislate their way out of a plastic bag doesn't mean they aren't gifted in other ways. When it comes to personal ambition and preservation, which is our interest here, these people are the best and the brightest, and so we must learn from them.

We are in awe that so many politicians can keep so many secrets under the radar for so long. Even with a 24-hour news cycle and cameras on every phone, these public figures manage to deflect, deny, distort, distract, and distance themselves from all manner of potential embarrassment. Their practices are to the political process, what camouflage and stealth are to the military in battle.

Some officials manage complex cover-ups for their entire professional lives. Governor Chris Christie comes to mind. The former mayor of Toronto, Mr. Ford, would be a notable exception. Most of these politicos manage to have affairs, take kickbacks, hide some income from the IRS, peddle some influence, and retire without a blemish (other than being a politician). You have to be gifted to be that duplicitous for a career. Some even make millions after their political careers with selective tell-all book deals and gratuitous lobbying jobs. Not bad work if you can get it.

If they can keep noisy skeletons out from under the microscope of the press, you can certainly keep yours beyond the faint oversight of your dim friends and relatives. If they can keep skeletons in Washington, you can learn to use their techniques to hide your secrets in Middle America.

Secrets Can Be Hidden in Plain Sight

Step back and admire political operatives as you would a preening peacock. Not only have elected officials and their minions perfected the art of spin and truth massage, they have also become highly proficient in the craft of concealing their more controversial ideas and actions. This professional capacity makes them well suited for keeping secrets in personal realms, and we consider them Master Teachers of The Skeleton Code.

We should, for instance, pay homage to the late former U.S. congressman from east Texas, Charlie Wilson. He knew The Skeleton Code before the name existed. To be elected to 12 terms in an ultra-conservative Bible-belt district while maintaining an extravagant playboy lifestyle is nothing short of awe-inspiring. We wish we could have interviewed him to get all his secrets about keeping secrets.

Yet there's more. Mr. Wilson didn't just keep a closet full of personal skeletons from his constituents; he didn't just manage his good-ol'-boy image back home. No, no. His genius went far beyond some simple dance of discretion or deception. Charlie did so much more! He kept secrets from the whole damn country. He managed to send billions of dollars, *secretly*, to Afghanistan to help national fighters deal with an invading Russian army.

Just think about that for a moment. How does one spend billions of taxpayer dollars without the American people knowing about it? How does one hide that much spending? OK, so maybe that's not so hard. In this case, however, we must also consider where the money went…to fund a secret operation against the Russians. Do you know how hard it is to keep a secret like that? This is a story of mythological proportions. No wonder they made it into a movie.

Politicians are truly the princes and princesses of pretense. Some may think they manipulate, but we prefer to think of them as "outcome engineers." Their primary outcome is to be reelected, and they are successful at this over 90% of the time. Compare that to the success of a professional baseball player at bat. It's impressive, especially given the contents of the typical political closet.

On the Other Hand

There are actually two types of political mentors: master secret keepers and master screw-ups. We should also learn from the latter. Consider Mitt Romney's 47% comment made at a private fundraiser in 2012 where he was unaware of being recorded. This was a classic debacle for his campaign, but a very teachable moment for the rest of us who want to avoid the same disaster. The walls have always had ears, but now they have eyes too. Orwell warned us about the possibility that Big Brother might one day be looking over our shoulders, but we should probably be more concerned about all our little friends and neighbors with cell phones!

As we hold up political masters for emulation, you may react by saying, "But what about all the scandals that come out of the political world? For being as smart as they are, politicians sure find creative ways to humiliate themselves!"

Granted. However, these political outings are dramatic precisely because they are rare and amplified by the media. It's the same phenomenon we see when there has been an airline crash or train derailment. The coverage is so intense and the images so raw, we come away thinking that airliners and trains are unsafe ways to move about, even though the opposite is true.

In reality, for every political scandal that hits the news there are thousands of skeletons that stay safely tucked away in their closets. Considering how much these power brokers are hiding and how much the media is looking, political figures are excellent secret keepers and worthy of respect, even though they suck at governing and legislating.

A Campaign Mindset

Jackie was the wife of a diplomat, living in an Arab country that shall remain nameless. Her two children went to a very nice private school where she was closely involved as a parent and volunteer. Both her husband's job and her role as a parent put her in social situations she would have preferred to avoid.

You see, Jackie was a card-carrying feminist and she hated every expression of male dominance and female submission she saw in her host culture. She could not stand to see the hijab and chafed every time she had to cover her head on an outing. She hated that Arab women were not included in the political discourse of their country. The fact that her father, a journalist, had been killed during the Six Day War at the explosive end of an Arab rocket probably colored her perspective.

Her hatred of her host culture was tempered slightly by her peace-loving husband, but only slightly. This meant she had to be a full-time actor worthy of an Oscar when she was in social situations. She tried to imagine how actress Meryl Streep would approach her "character."

She also maintained her cover by creating the fantasy of a political campaign. In other words, she mimicked the masters. Whenever she encountered Arab men, she was on the campaign trail. She loved the lies and the power surge of grand manipulation—telling people what they wanted to hear, which was just the opposite of what she actually felt. It became her way of becoming a smiling assassin. In her fantasy, she was insulting them with contrived kindness and getting no small measure of satisfaction doing so.

We regret her one-dimensional view of Arab culture, but appreciate such a masterful touch, and a great strategy for keeping a very potent secret. We also share the story because we know you have enemies as well. There are people in your social circles that you despise, and yet you cannot let this be known. Maybe it's your boss's wife or your husband's mother.

Make it a political campaign. Imagine that you're seeking votes from the people you despise. Imagine the cameras are rolling and an Emmy is on the line. You can do this. Just give yourself permission to play the part and imitate the masters.

Twain discovered this truth long ago and said, *It's easier to fool people than to convince them that they have been fooled.* What a gift this is! If you want to mimic the masters, then master these basic political skills:

1. Propaganda (Spin)

We agree with this famous Bush-ism: "You can fool some of the people all the time, and those are the ones you want to concentrate on." Propaganda is an excellent tool to accomplish this. The term may have some negative connotations for you, so let us help with that. We all know how propaganda is used in communist, fascist, or theocratic regimes to oppress and control. However, you need not stoop to this depraved version when a more refined and advantageous expression is available. It's called *Spin*.

Propaganda is the art of swaying public opinion, even if your public is limited to your family and closest friends. It is nothing more than emphasizing one narrative, one perspective, one notion, so that others seem less plausible or downright ridiculous. If this messaging is repeated often enough, with enough conviction, you'll begin to believe it yourself. This is a good measure of how it's working on others.

Spin is admittedly a form of propaganda that can be immensely irritating when it comes from a politician you find contemptible. Don't let that put you off. It's much more palatable when it works for you, and of course, you'll be using it only to maintain your privacy and not to undermine the political process of your country (we hope).

Remember that spinning is a creative movement used in many dances and by world-class athletes. Enjoy spin like you would a good tango or a triple axel. When your life is a moving target, it's more difficult for others to pin you down.

Spinning is also a common movement in child's play, and if you watch the masters, you can see that they are often being playful with their words and actions. This is in contrast to their personal backstabbing strategy.

Humor and lightheartedness will often make you more believable and likeable, like Charlie Wilson. Practice these two vital assets used by masters who are spinning away from their secrets.

Spin, we should emphasize, is not blatant untruth, though some less experienced spinners default to that practice. The best spin is true as far as it goes, even if it doesn't go that far. We think of it as weighted truth. When you spin to keep a secret, you are simply shifting the balance of believability in the direction of your benefit. You just need to tip the scale, not bottom it out. Think of your spin as an alternative perspective. In our culture, all perspectives should be heard, right? Make your perspective work for you in managing your skeletons.

2. Cherry Picking

Facts can be frustrating, especially when they conspire to crack your closet door or complicate your preferred story. We do not want to be victimized by the syndrome called "analysis paralysis" where we are overwhelmed by so much information we cannot act in our best interest. The art of protecting skeletons requires the selective use of information, often called "cherry picking." There are two primary strategies in cherry picking that will be advantageous to you.

First, you must be especially careful to utilize only the most leading information available—leading away from your closet, of course. When you are covering your tracks, make sure your alibi contains only the essential elements of the story. Many nervous types overdo the explanation, which raises, rather than lowers, suspicion. Give select information in a casual way and move on to something that will be more interesting to the listener.

Second, seasoned cherry picking requires the careful selection of information to be withheld. This is not legal in every situation. For instance, the SEC has truthfulness standards for companies that advertise investment products. These laws not only dictate how accurate information must be, but also protect potential investors from the deceptive omission of information. Investment companies cannot be deceptive in what they say, or in what they fail to say. If this were the standard in Washington, there would be no speech.

Thank goodness the SEC has no power to protect anyone from carefully chosen omissions about your personal life. The most effective strategies of misinformation make the most of these key omissions in shaping the story. Cherry picking allows you to believe the stories you are telling as far as you tell them. What an asset.

Frank contracted a sexually transmitted infection from a one-night stand and didn't want to risk infecting his wife or telling the secret. Thankfully, he had studied political science and had worked on a political campaign, so he was familiar with cherry picking. He told his wife that he had been to the doctor (true statement). He told her that he had a "plumbing problem" that was embarrassing (also true). When she pressed out of concern, he told her it was the infamous "erectile dysfunction," which was also true in a sense.

Not only did Frank do a great job cherry picking to protect his skeleton, he gave his wife something she wanted in the process—a husband who wouldn't be bothering her. He could see her smiling as she walked away from the conversation. Now that's political polish and a win-win. All Frank has to do now is keep the pills out of sight.

3. Find Good Supporting Actors

You know those satisfied customers you see touting a product on TV? How about the concerned citizen sharing their opinion in a political ad? They sure sound believable and sincere, don't they? Yet they are actors who get paid for playing a part and saying things that others tell them to say. Americans are trained to respond positively to these messages like Pavlov ringing the bell for his dogs. It's all very convincing and effective, worthy of any aspiring Don Draper.

This is a marketing technique turned political strategy that you can use without paying anyone. And you never have to say, "I approved this message."

A third party can often make a more convincing assertion about you than you can make about yourself. An "objective" person can offer a denial or defense for you that doesn't feel like either. While there are risks involved, the potential benefits of using a spokesperson to guard your skeletons can be substantial.

Friends are the best option for this work because they will often cooperate without prying. Find a friend without skeletons because that means they are hiding their own very well and are probably already adept at story telling. These personal spokespersons don't have to be the bleeding heart type as long as they are believable. In the right setting, let them know how some swirling (untrue) suspicion about you is causing you to need Prozac. They will be happy to intercede on your behalf to set the record straight. This is pure gold if the friend is chosen well. Co-workers or neighbors require more manipulation, which adds to the risk.

Their marketing approach should be short and simple as in the following:

"Look...I know Karen. She's not perfect but she's a decent person. There's no way she had a one-night stand on that business trip."

"I've known Bob for years. I've been on golf trips with him. We work out at the same gym. If he wore women's underwear, I would have picked up on that along the way."

"Tasha teaches school and volunteers at the soup kitchen. The district wouldn't have hired her if she worked for the KGB."

Don't wait for a crisis to look for a good supporting actor. Develop the asset now. Look for opportunities to defend the person with potential. Stand up for someone at work and let him or her know it. Squelch the rumor during a party, with humility of course. When you need their support, they will be ready and willing to give it.

4. Use Straw Skeletons

Politicians who stay in office develop excellent misdirection skills, and these same skills can also help you keep your secrets. Elected leaders must learn how to deflect attention from their own absurd positions, as well as their lack of effectiveness. They do this primarily by creating caricatures of their opponents and/or their positions, and then attacking those caricatures. This is the classic Straw Man technique.

Candidate Donald Trump did this as well as anyone in the run-up to the 2016 election. When Jeb Bush attacked one of Trump's positions, "The Donald" would say that Bush was a "low-energy" candidate and the press would zero in on Bush's energy instead of Trump's policy. When asked to spell out his views on immigration, Mr. Trump would warn his audience that all those rapists and murderers coming to this country illegally had to be stopped. In the whiplash that followed his words, the conversation shifted away from Trump's actual ideas on immigration.

Trump made some of the most outlandish deflections ever made in a campaign and rather than being dismissed, he was embraced as a real candidate willing to say what he thought. No candidate in recent history has done a better job moving attention away from his inexperience and lack of substance to the deficiencies of his opponents.

The straw skeleton is brilliant stagecraft; especially in the way it shifts attention to the imagined and exaggerated faults and fallacies of others. It works like a charm when you're dealing with people who need a scapegoat, turning their negative energy toward your enemy or convenient straw skeleton. 90% of all campaign rhetoric is some form of straw man argument or scapegoating. History is filled with "fall guys" (and girls) who were fired after their political bosses felt the heat of some scandal. It usually works.

When crafting a straw skeleton to divert attention from your secret, keep these strategies in mind:

- Choose a diversionary person carefully:
    o Someone likely to be hiding a similar skeleton as your own.
    o Someone who could stand to be knocked down a notch.
    o Someone with larger likeability issues.
    o Someone with tendencies to be overly defensive.
- Choose your diversionary issue carefully:
    o Those trying to expose your skeleton may have a particular appetite for a specific indiscretion; not just any substitute will do.
    o Keep your straw issue on the same level as your own secret; don't use suspicion about tax evasion to cover the fact that you bounce checks on a regular basis.
    o Keep it focused; you don't need to divert everyone; only those who may be getting too close to your own closet.

Humans have an appetite for judgment, but aren't usually particular about who satisfies that need. If you don't want their talons in you, give them someone else or something else that tastes even better. Choose your straw skeletons well and in addition to the deflection, you may learn a political skill that could come in handy if you ever run for office.

5. Try Fogging

When your skeleton is partially exposed, you will need to move with skill and speed to limit the damage and re-secure your closet. Often the best course of action is a technique called *fogging*.

Jack and Joanne were having yet another argument over where all the money was going. A check had bounced and the budget was not working. Jack had a gambling problem, but had convinced Joanne that he was using funds to help take care of his elderly mother. When Joanne saw the bank statement and how their savings account was almost depleted, she went ballistic.

But instead of meeting her head-on, as most guilty people would, or as if he were standing on some moral high ground by taking care of Mom, he used the fogging technique. It went like this:

"You know, honey, you're right and I'm sorry. I've been too focused on being the dutiful son instead of the providing husband. I know how much the money shortage makes you crazy and it's just really difficult for me right now, but I know I can do better."

Suddenly, Joanne was completely off her original plan of attack. Jack had just taken most of the wind out of her sails. She dropped her raised sword down to her side and soon it would be back in its sheath. One more admission and she'd start feeling sorry for the man she was about to kill.

Use fogging when you know your skeleton has been compromised to some degree—when denial will only dig you deeper and make the fall further.

> When you are attacked or accused, you give the suspicious or angry person a soft target instead of a full frontal defense.

The strategy of fogging will seem familiar to those who have trained in judo or a similar discipline. Fogging, like judo, uses the movement of an attacker as leverage for defense. The technique removes the hard target an aggressor expects, replacing it with "fog."

When you are attacked or accused, you give the suspicious or angry person a soft target instead of a full frontal defense. The latter always escalates the situation and frequently fully outs your secret in the process. Fogging, on the other hand, because it is a partial admission with apology, immediately puts your opponent off balance. If they punch, they will be punching air. You give them a little win as soon as the confrontation begins, and they are less likely to pursue you like an assassin.

Here is another example:

"You were talking to Samantha again, weren't you? You promised you'd never do that again."

"Yes, I was and I'm sorry to upset you. She called me because she found some old running shoes of mine and wondered if I wanted them. I told her I didn't, so that was it."

Or this…

"You knew I was going to be fired and you didn't tell me. I thought we were friends!"

"Yes, I did know. I'm sorry. I've been trying to get HR to reconsider, but I failed. I was hoping they would change their minds."

Or this…

"You lying SOB. You told me you had quit collecting music boxes. The whole house is filled with those things!"

"You have every right to be angry. I have been going to the Music Box Anonymous meetings, but I lapsed when I saw that Boite a Musique."

6. Find The Loopholes

Politics, law and life are filled with loopholes. There are always loopholes that can work to your advantage if you find them and use them effectively. To do this is a masterstroke of genius.

Ken remembers being introduced to the concept of loopholes. Chuck told him he would give him a dollar if he jumped off the top of the monkey bars in the school playground. This was the 4th grade 50 years ago, so we are talking serious money.

"Let me see the dollar," Ken said.

He showed him the bill.

"You swear?" Ken asked.

"I swear," he said.

So Ken climbed to the top of those monkey bars and looked down. "Do you have two dollars?" he asked, regretting his impulse. Ken was petrified. But hey, OSHA wouldn't allow a monkey bar design to be so high that anyone could get hurt, right? Or was that before OSHA?

By this time several kids were gathered around, so Ken had to jump or be humiliated. He did. It hurt his knee, which is still the reason he can't break par in golf. Got all dirty too, but that was a perk. Jenny asked if he was OK, which was a double perk.

Ken dusted himself off, worked hard to make it seem like nothing, and put his hand out for the prize. That's when Chuck grinned and extended the hand that had been behind his back with his fingers crossed.

"I had my fingers crossed, you dummy," he laughed. Then he made sure everyone else enjoyed the joke. That's when the bell rung and everyone headed back to class.

Ken's friend Billy stuck around and explained it. "It's like April Fool's," he said. "The normal laws of truth are suspended when you cross your fingers."

And so it is with loopholes.

We will not expand on the practice here, but if you want to know how a master uses loopholes, consider how big business uses tax law and how politicians deal with political contributions. They learn how to work the system for self-enrichment while skirting the legal definition of bribery or tax evasion. This is why many large donations to PACs can be done anonymously. You cannot give directly to a PAC and protect your identity, but a loophole allows corporations or individual donors to funnel their donations through 501(c)4 "social welfare" organizations. These organizations do not have to identify donors. Brilliant. If you have the money, you can buy your election discreetly.

Loopholes are advantageous for protecting active secrets. If you sit quietly in the lotus position, these loopholes will often appear to you out of nowhere. Attorney friends are also insightful about creative options to most circumstances, but they often come with a hefty bill. You may find a completely new loophole to keep your closet collection to a minimum.

Your old secrets may also benefit from loopholes. If you don't want to tell future partners about the alimony you're paying, try adding a confidentiality clause in the separation agreement. If you don't want a future spouse to check on your purchases, get that private credit card and P.O. Box now. Don't leave your loophole unclaimed.

Note: a poor loophole is better than none at all.

7. Use the Red Button Getaway

Jet pilots have ejection seats. Dopers have a nearby toilet that actually flushes. Farmers in Oklahoma have tornado shelters. And the president always has a dozen ways to get out of trouble with lightning speed, including a really cool escape pod from Air Force One. Speed can be your best friend when you are surprised by a closet failure. A quick response will keep your adversaries off-balance. Those who stumble and bumble their way into an explanation might as well post their confession on YouTube. This old story makes the point:

One day a wife was sitting by the river sewing when her thimble slipped into the water. When she cried out, an angel appeared and asked why she was crying. She told the angel that she had dropped her thimble in the river and needed it to make a living for her family.

The angel reached down into the waters and pulled out a thimble made of pure gold with pearls.

"Is this it?"

"No," said the wife, honestly.

So the angel reached in again and pulled out a silver thimble ringed with sapphires.

"Is this it?"

"No, I'm afraid not."

So the angel reached in again and pulled out a plain leather thimble.

"Is this yours?"

"O yes, thank you," said the woman as she bowed.

The angel, pleased with the woman's honesty, gave her all three thimbles to keep, and this was a great blessing to her family because they were poor.

Some time later, the woman was walking along that same river with her husband when all of sudden he fell in and disappeared beneath the water. The woman cried out again and the same angel appeared.

"Why are you crying," the angel asked?

"My husband has fallen into the river and our family can't possibly survive without him," she wailed.

So the angel reached into the river and pulled out a man who looked very much like Brad Pitt.

"Is this your husband?"

"Why yes it is," said the woman with delight.

"Aha," replied the angel. "You have lied. This is not your husband."

The woman bowed and said, "Please forgive me. This is a misunderstanding. You see, if I had answered 'no' to your question, you would have reached into the river and pulled out someone who looked like Matthew McConaughey. Then, when I told you he wasn't my husband, you would have come up with my real husband and then given all three men to me because of my honesty. But there's no way I could take care of all three men, so that's why I said yes to the first very attractive one."

The ancient moral of this story is, according to the sages, "whenever a woman lies, it's for a good and honorable reason, and in the best interest of others." We also consider it a great example of the quick, evasive and effective reply of a master secret-keeper.

Remember what's at stake if your secret gets out. If you don't learn from the best, you could suffer with the rest, like former political insider turned journalist George Stephanopoulos. As it turns out, the former Clinton aide's secret was a very large donation he had made to the Clinton Foundation—nothing illegal mind you, but something that would cast doubt on his objectivity in reporting on the Clintons.

Sadly, George lived among the political elite, but didn't learn his lessons from them. He interviewed a critic of the foundation without offering full disclosure of the conflict. His journalistic reputation took a blow and he had to join many of his old political colleagues on the apology bandwagon.

Remember those immortal words penned by Shakespeare:

All the world is a stage, and all the men and women merely players; they have their exits and their entrances; and one man in his time plays many parts.

Play the part of a political master, and you'll be able to live a life of delightful duplicity, all to your advantage.

In summary, to become a master secret keeper:

- Relate to people like you're running for office.
- Imagine yourself playing the roll of an accomplished politico.
- Learn the art of Spin.
- Cherry pick your information and your omissions.
- Enlist a supporting actor to cover your bases.
- Develop your straw skeletons.

- Try fogging when you are caught in a pinch.
- Be proactive in your search for loopholes.
- Finally, create some quick escape routes.

As Ambrose Bierce said, politics is "the conduct of public affairs for private advantage." So is The Skeleton Code. You too can have this advantage by learning from the masters.

Chapter Three

Take The Offensive

There is no great genius without a mixture of madness.
—Aristotle

We suggest developing your own skeleton protection plan in the same order we present the strategies in this book. Don't start on the offensive. Begin with chapter one to ensure you are dressed for success. Adopting techniques from the political masters in chapter two will help you embrace the new offensive strategies in this chapter.

A reporter who idolized the great golfer Jack Nicholas was chosen at random to interview the star. "You really are the greatest to play the game," the reporter said. "I'm particularly impressed with your ability to make your way around a course. You just seem to know where you're going. What's your secret?"

The Bear thought for a moment and then with a straight face said, "The holes are numbered."

Unlike a golf course, the code is not as sequential as 1-18. Even so, there are some clear offensive strategies you can use to get yourself around the course of life—past the hazards of exposure and in control of your persona. The steps aren't numbered, but they are reachable and they do relate to one another. In fact, many of the same strategies that make you successful in other life ventures will help you achieve good skeleton maintenance.

Yet, we have to be honest with you. As Aristotle said, you're going to need a little madness to be a genius at keeping your secrets safe. You have to be a little crazy to play this game anyway, so use your outlandish inclinations to your advantage.

In this chapter, we will help you take the offensive in skeleton security instead of always feeling like you are back on your heels playing defense. We will also share some of our 90/10 insights and strategies that will help move you toward an impressive and successful persona.

Secrets Will Pop Up On You

You may think it's better to let secrets and sleeping dogs lie. You may think that the longer they have been in your closet, the less threatening they are. Think again.

When Ken was 5 or 6 years old, Santa brought him a childhood punching bag for Christmas. It was an inflatable clown about four feet tall—just about Ken's height at the time. It had some sand in the bottom that made it stand up straight and return to that position when you hit it.

Maybe his parents thought Ken needed to vent some energy or aggression. Or maybe, since he was the punching bag for his older brother, they thought he needed someone or something to serve the same purpose.

After it was inflated that Christmas morning, Ken gave it a whack and it went all the way down to the floor. As he looked over at his dad for affirmation, that damn clown bounced back and smacked him right in the face. He was stunned.

When his dad saw that Ken was about to cry, the father got down on his knees, punched the clown and let it bounce back and hit him in the face. Then he fell to the floor like it had knocked him down. It was pretty funny to see his dad knocked over by a goofy clown, so Ken decided to laugh instead of cry, though he continued to have a love/hate relationship with that clown.

Don't be fooled. Skeletons will come back at you just like that, and they will probably be smiling just like that stupid clown. No matter how goofy they look in your closet; no matter how much hot air they contain; no matter how benign or playful they seem; they will, without warning, come up and punch you right between the eyes! That's why you need an excellent offensive game plan!

Defense Is Not Enough

Everyone in sports knows that a good offense is as important as a good defense. If you put enough points on the board, your defense doesn't have to be that good. This is even truer when it comes to keeping secrets safe.

It's not enough to bury the past and walk away. There are too many people with shovels who like to dig in your dirt. *There are too*

> It's not enough to bury the past and walk away. There are too many people with shovels who like to dig in your dirt.

many prying eyes. It's not enough to tuck away the untidy family secret when one drink too many will un-tuck it in a hurry.

Defensive strategies for skeleton maintenance are never going to succeed in the long term because some people never sleep. When they do sleep, snoopy people eventually wake up and get suspicious for breakfast. Their favorite pastime is to pry into your life for some reason or no reason at all. Whether you know it or not, there is at least one person in your life who is your personal paparazzi. You can't sit around waiting for these blowhards to blow your cover. You have to take the offensive.

When Defense Is Too Little Too Late

Sandy was a rising star in the state chapter of her family values coalition and had aspirations to one day lead the national organization, a platform from which she could make millions in speaking engagements and book sales.

At age 29, Sandy was elected to serve on the national executive committee, which created some jealousy in some of the older men who were bypassed. Because she had so little competition for promotion in her state, she never experienced the intense nature of a national campaign. For a non-profit, these elections for office could become pretty negative. Sandy's inexperience made her complacent when she was eventually nominated to lead the national organization, even though she faced an older and more desperate challenger for the office.

It had been 25 years since Sandy was involved in a youthful indiscretion from her college days—an arrest for having 2 ounces of marijuana in her car. She had forgotten about it. This is a fatal flaw in skeleton security that we see far too often. Because our skeleton does not terrorize us on a regular basis, we think it will never go out and annihilate our reputation.

Sadly, Sandy's challenger for the position discovered what was in her closet and found the mug shot that told the story better than he could. The news and the photo rocked the sensibilities of the values organization, and Sandy's opponent didn't even need to comment. He just let the story and suffering unfold.

Sandy tried to apologize and explain, but many of her supporters were too shocked and saddened to attend the convention and vote. They felt betrayed and, of course, self-satisfied in their judgment. She lost the election and her dream.

Sandy should have gone on the offensive to guard her closet instead of trusting the passage of time and the apathy of opponents. She could have been proactive in at least two ways. She might have been able to have her record expunged, as have many before her. Or, if she could not do that, she could have turned a milder form of her closeted skeleton into a knight in shining armor. Let us explain.

Skelton Immunology

As Edward Jenner and others discovered, the human body can develop an immunity to some diseases by being exposed to less virulent strains of the disease. We use the same "vaccination" strategy to help others become immune to their problematic skeletons. While this treatment does not work with every disease or every secret, it may work with yours. With the right finesse and wisdom, you can divulge just enough of a secret to render the real one almost harmless.

Sandy could have taken the offensive and used this form of skeleton immunology. She should have told her story of infrequent pot use early in her career at the non-profit. This would have allowed her to control the narrative, something she could not do when she was out-ed later on. She could have expressed great remorse for her immaturity and described how she had come to her senses and turned her life around.

Values activists in her organization would have loved that stuff. Then, she could have used the experience as a catalyst for a personal crusade to keep pot illegal, a position that would have given her even more capital in her organization. Who better to carry this banner than someone who had been 'abused' by the drug?

Righteous indignation about your own secrets can be an effective offensive strategy. Simply attack the weakness you are hiding, without getting into gory details. Again, not every skeleton can become such a public asset, though every closet needs a good offensive plan. Had Sandy played offense like this, her closet would have been almost bulletproof. If you want that type of security, read on.

Good Rules of Offense

Steven Wright famously said that *42.7% of all statistics are made up on the spot*. We think the number is closer to 73.4. However, we have worked through many of these extraneous stats in order to help you develop the best offensive secret keeping strategy available.

We do seem to be a culture captivated by percentages and chances: from returns on investments to mortgage rates to batting averages to the discount we get on new shoes. Everywhere we go, in just about every self help book we read, we run into some form of the 90/10 Rule. Given how many of these rubrics are applied to every aspect of life, there must be a 90/10 dimension to the universe.

One of these rules states that life is 10% what happens to you and 90% what you do about it. There is likely some truth to this perspective. We know a woman who inherited 90 Grand, and in less than a year of shopping, there was only 10 thousand left. Some argue that 90% of the economic and political power in this country is controlled by 10% of the population. We see the pattern, but we would like to be in that 10%, without any of the power or responsibility.

We have found that 90/10 equations impart some real wisdom that is applicable to secret keeping. Here are two 90/10 rules that will help you take the offensive in pursuit of your pretense:

1. 90% of your problems come from the bottom 10% of your secrets.

As a matter of discretion and personal privacy, we all keep secrets from others. We would not lose sleep if 90% of these secrets were shared or uncovered. Susie decided to get breast implants because she could never find a dress or swimsuit that fit, and she was tired of padded bras. The augmentation was very proportional. She didn't want to look like Barbie.

The modest change helped her keep the procedure confidential, which fit her private personality. She intended to keep it that way. She hadn't even told her closest friends.

However, if they did find out, it would not be a huge deal. She would explain her reasons for the procedure and the secrecy and no one, including herself, would lose any sleep over it. 90% of our secrets are like this.

However, at the bottom of the proverbial inverted iceberg is that 10% of our closet that we must manage and maintain at all costs. This is the 10% of our private world that would suck almost 100% of the life right out of us if it were exposed. These are the secrets that would make your friends change their phone numbers and email addresses. There are no shades of grey with these skeletons. They will black out your universe. Devise your offensive strategy with this 10% in mind.

Additionally, there is another 90/10 Skeleton Code rule you should respect:

2. 90% of the people in your life have less than a 10% interest in your personal life.

Sometimes life is kind. 90% of the people in your life will miss your skeletons even if they flash right in front of them. They just won't be looking. They will be too preoccupied to overhear the gossip in the coffee room. They will be too busy to notice that your eyes are bloodshot.

On average, 90% of the people in your life are never going to be even casual friends. They are little moons orbiting your personal planet with their own secrets and struggles. They have a natural apathy toward you and your circumstances, which is a very admirable trait. You can feel more relaxed around these people because they represent only about 10% of your overall closet risk.

Some of this 90% might find it surprising or mildly disgusting that you've collected your nail clippings in glass jars since you were 18. That is pretty weird. Yet because they don't really care to know much about you, they will probably create a mental block about that interesting facet of your life. On the other hand, the guy you're dating will likely find the nearest exit available.

Your next-door neighbor might be amused that you are growing peyote in some backyard pots, but she's not going to report it or get worked up about it, especially if you share. She's one-sixteenth Cherokee and thinks it might help her get in touch with her ancestors. In the 10% camp, however, is your busybody cousin who could turn your prickly plant into the worst thorny disaster ever to befall your devout family.

This 90/10 rule does not apply in every case. The pivotal issue is whether the 90-percent-er is directly affected or not. If you're sex-ting that casual neighbor's spouse, she will quickly move from 90 to 10 to 1 of your worst nightmares.

When planning a good offense, focus your efforts on those 10% people who are most interested in your closet.

Still not sure you need an offensive strategy? Then why not score yourself on our Social Performance Scale? The more points you put up here, the more you need a good offense.

Social Performance Scale

Directions: Place an "X" at the appropriate place along the continuum and add your scores.

1. My coarse humor and language would make Dick Cheney blush.

Never   Hardly Ever   Sometimes   Regularly   Can't Stop

1_____ 2_____3 _____4 _____ 5 _____ 6_____7

2. Lil' Wayne listens to my sexual innuendo for lyric ideas.
Never   Hardly Ever   Sometimes   Regularly   Can't Stop

1_____ 2_____3 _____4 _____ 5 _____ 6_____7

3. My wardrobe, mannerisms, language, and eyes scream, "I'm a junkie."
Never   Hardly Ever   Sometimes   Regularly   Can't Stop

1_____ 2_____3 _____4 _____ 5 _____ 6_____7

4. My commentary on religion sends the ACLU to DEFCON 5.
Never   Hardly Ever   Sometimes   Regularly   Can't Stop

1_____ 2_____3 _____4 _____ 5 _____ 6_____7

5. My racial slurs would make MLK choose violence.
Never   Hardly Ever   Sometimes   Regularly   Can't Stop

1_____ 2_____3 _____4 _____ 5 _____ 6_____7

6. Tequila makes my clothes fall off.
Never   Hardly Ever   Sometimes   Regularly   Can't Stop

1_____ 2_____3 _____4 _____ 5 _____ 6_____7

7. My treatment of animals has put me on the SPCA's "Most Wanted" list.

Never   Hardly Ever   Sometimes   Regularly   Can't Stop

1_____ 2_____3 _____4 _____5 _____ 6_____7

<u>Scoring</u>:

7-14   The Makings of a Good Offense
15-28   Some Bad Plays Are Holding You Back
29-35   Some Serious Social Skid-Marking
36+   Just Plain Offensive

Time To Get Serious

We hope we have convinced you of the need to have an offensive strategy. With that established, let's now take the time to outline some practice drills to help take your game to a new level.

1. Practice Visualization

Great athletes and successful entrepreneurs understand and practice the art of visualization. They see the shot before they take it. They create the headline about their success and put it up on their wall so they see it every day. This process taps into their conscious and subconscious energy, preparing them to function at a peak level.

This strategy works equally well for those who want to be excellent secret-keepers and maintain the integrity of their closets. There are two primary dimensions to this art of visualization.

First, you must visualize the person you want others to see—your airbrushed self. Photographers can put a digital image into Photoshop or Portrait Pro software and remove every blemish. They can tone curves, color lips, fill out thinning hair, and brighten eyes. Now, visualize the same process for your character! How do you want people to see you in terms of character and personality? If you can't visualize it, no one else will be able to either.

How do you want people to see you in terms of character and personality? If you can't visualize it, no one else will be able to either.

We highly recommend establishing your persona on social media, but also warn you to refrain from all but the most benign posts. Spend your time "liking" videos of cute animals or saying Happy Birthday to friends. No Political Posts! Don't Engage in Culture War! Neutral is Natural!

Visualize your offense and your success. Many find that trophies, certificates, and other "awards" are helpful as they imagine their best self.

Amanda had some very self-centered secrets and wanted to present herself as someone who cared about others. She purchased a very nice plaque declaring that she was the Volunteer of the Year at a medical center in the city where she had lived. She hung it behind her desk so that she, and others, could visualize her as a woman of deep compassion.

We know some very successful people who have done the same with trophies or certificates.

When others notice your visual props, it's important to feign humility, especially when your "awards" are for humanitarian pursuits. Remember, their purpose is to help you visualize your preferred persona. They represent some aspiration that serves you well. They balance out your life when it is tilted too far in a difficult direction. If your visuals happen to make a positive impression on others, consider it a bonus.

The second dimension of visualization that will help you be proactive in skeleton maintenance can be both pleasant and disturbing. It is important that you take time to picture the demise of others whose skeletons have escaped. We discuss this more in the chapter called *Fear Failure*.

To help you imagine what you must avoid at all costs, take some time to search the Internet for people who have been shamed, embarrassed, or ruined because of their exposure. This can be a pleasant pastime. There is an odd but compelling satisfaction when you see someone else haunted and hung by the same skeletons you're hiding. Yet pleasure and amusement are not the goals of this exercise.

We want you to visualize disaster so that you can avoid it in your own life. There are many others in this world who are hiding the same skeletons that populate your closet. When they don't follow the Code, they get busted. Read these stories. Imagine being in the shoes of someone whose life has been turned upside down. Envision the shame and embarrassment of those who failed to take the offensive and suffered the consequences. Bookmark the stories for later reference and revisit them when you are feeling a bit too smug and secure. They will help you picture the place you never want to go.

The path of failure is well-worn and tragic: Embarrassment and shame leads to withdrawal, which leads to loneliness, which leads to eating comfort food, which leads to higher cholesterol, which leads to plaque, which leads to myocardial infarctions, which leads to... well, you know.

2. Stay Focused

Woody Allen said that *90% of success is just showing up*, but we have found that you can't create a great offense for guarding secrets if your mind is occupied elsewhere. You have to show up <u>and</u> suit up.

Successful people learn how to overcome their Attention Deficit Disorders, especially when they are under the pressure of hiding something. If you are going to be successful at skeleton maintenance, you will need the discipline called *focus*. You can be "out to lunch" with your friends, but not about your secrets.

Janice had never been so upset in her life. She had hoped to meet a great guy in college and Trace seemed to be the one. Their relationship was moving along nicely when it was suddenly broadsided by that conniving "_____" Dexie. I mean, what kind of name is Dexie anyway?!

The more Dexie flirted with Trace, the more irritated and possessive Janice became. Not surprisingly, this drove Trace away and into the welcoming arms of that stupid "_____."

Strange and frightening things happen in otherwise normal brains when they are enraged. The emotions usually shut down the higher-functioning processes we depend on to make wise decisions. Crashing into another car because the other driver cut you off is an example of this kind of reckless rage.

Janice felt this kind of rage, and it was not a passing passion. She stewed in it for days after Trace broke things off. She was obsessed with what she could do to hurt Dexie. She decided that fire was the right weapon, given that she wanted Dexie to burn in hell. There was a loveseat on Dexie's apartment deck where she and Trace would sit and cuddle. Janice had actually seen this. So she determined that she would set the furniture on fire, hoping the smoke would get into Dexie's apartment and ruin her clothes. The thought that the fire might spread to the apartment never registered. Like we said, rage turns off other brain processes.

Janice's plan worked just as she imagined, except that the fire on the deck spread to the apartment wall before the fire department could arrive, doing significant damage to the unit. It was ruled arson, but another suspect had drawn the interest of the police. Janice was left huddling in fear before she transferred to another school, taking the secret with her.

Strong emotions are the worst enemy of mental focus. You can create secrets without focus, but you can't guard them without that discipline.

This is the reason you must develop a Skeleton Code offense when you are reasonable, rather than when you are under duress or pressure.

Albert Einstein was searching for a paper clip. With his assistant's help, he located one, but it was bent beyond use. While they were searching for a tool to fix the clip, the assistant found a box of paper clips. Einstein took out a new paper clip and began fashioning a tool that would straighten out the first paper clip. His assistant asked why he didn't simply use one of the good paper clips and discard the bent one. Einstein replied, "Once I am set on a goal, it becomes difficult to deflect me."

This is the focus and discipline needed to become a master secret-keeper. You simply cannot be deflected from that goal. Taking the offensive is not a part-time job. It is not for the half-hearted.

3. Spend 90% of your time with people who know less than 10% of your story.

The law of averages is consistent most of the time. The more you play with fire, the more you're likely to get burned. Close friends and family discover secrets 90 times more often than even the most curious bystander.

To reduce the risk of skeleton exposure, you should spend more time with people who have the least access to your life. Sure, they are boring or self-absorbed and you'd rather wear sandpaper underwear, but this is a great advantage. You can relax more around morons. Unless they have pathological tendencies, they are not likely to dig into your past or your present. In their minds, they know little about you for good reason. Maybe you're not that interesting to them, or maybe they have a truckload of skeletons they're hiding from you and will keep good distance.

Jerry loves to play golf, and he does that with friends every now and then. Most of the time, however, he goes solo and gets matched with a group where he doesn't know anyone. Sometimes there's a real jerk in the mix, but usually the company is cordial, superficial, and done after four or five hours.

This suits Jerry just fine. He suffers from Pemphigus vulgaris, which produces blistering and sores on the skin. He never knows what his skin might do, and the look is pretty disgusting. Most people assume it's an STD or Ebola and they get very uncomfortable. So it works better for Jerry to spend his time with strangers. He could care less what they think.

4. Practice Perseveration

You may be familiar with a condition psychologists call *perseveration*. If you are not, you probably recognize that it comes from the same root as the word *persevere*. Perseveration is perseverance on steroids. It is the continuation of an action beyond a reasonable point. It is fixation on a goal or action that renders one incapable or unwilling to evaluate the appropriateness of such action. So it's perfect for skeleton maintenance.

You've already decided to keep the secret. You don't need to be distracted by questions of reasonableness or appropriateness. Therefore, it's better to be focused 110% on your goal.

In the movie *Tin Cup*, the main character, played by Kevin Costner, is so fixated on reaching a par-5 green in two shots that he blocks out all negative outcomes like losing. Even though he hits several balls in the water, he wins the girl and becomes famous. All because he practiced *perseveration*, a final ingredient in your move from skeleton defense to skeleton offense.

Learn to Sidestep

MIT is one of the finest universities in the world. What are the chances that someone could work there for 28 years, including serving as a dean, with a completely bogus academic history? Well, that's what Marilee Jones pulled off until the university realized she had never actually earned the undergraduate or master's degrees that adorned her resume. Ms. Jones actually had not earned any college degrees at all.

While we might admire her raw courage and her ability to hide such an imposing skeleton for so many years, we should also state that The Code would have saved her a great deal of heartache. Had Ms. Jones understood our principles of a good offense, she would have realized what a low percentage game she was playing. She would have had better odds at the roulette wheel in Caesar's Palace.

What she could have done was use the MIT experience as a stepping stone out of the spotlight and into a less conspicuous environment. There are just too many credential hawks in the rarified air of schools like MIT. Once she had a foothold at MIT, she could have written a ticket anywhere. A sidestep move could have taken her to greater heights in less conspicuous environs. Who knows? She may have become a college president, which sure beats becoming a pariah.

Don't wait for someone to score on your skeletons. Take bold moves to protect your closet. When it comes to keeping your secrets safe, don't worry about what's right. Worry about what's left, as in what's left of your good name and reputation! Your future depends on secure secrets. You can't be satisfied with passive restraint when it comes to skeletons. Those boney boys are active—sometimes radioactive!

Remember, a great offensive game plan will include the following:

- Take your skeletons seriously. They are working even when you're not.
- Playing closet defense is not good enough.
- Prepare a great offense before you need a defense.

- Build your offense to protect you from the deepest 10% of your closet and the nearest 10% of your relationships.
- Strengthen your offense with visualization, focus, relationship management, and perseveration.

Chapter Four

Fear Failure

Always do what you're afraid to do.
—Ralph Waldo Emerson

A s you are gaining new insights and devising new plans to keep your secrets safe, you will also need enough motivation to fuel these new ventures. Dressing for success is not a temporary tactic, nor is learning from political masters or creating a great offense. Skeleton security is a long-distance race and you will need to find a substantial motivational fuel supply to persevere in this contest.

Fear is the oldest and best motivator known to humanity. Coaches, drill sergeants, and mothers have used it effectively for centuries. In other areas of life, perhaps, fear can be a liability, but not when it comes to personal security. Fear can work for you and that's what we're proposing in this chapter.

Fear is the oldest and best motivator known to humanity. Coaches, drill sergeants, and mothers have used it effectively for centuries.

We found a board game a few years ago that is both fun and interesting. It's called *Worst Case Scenario* and it tests your knowledge about how to survive in difficult and dangerous situations. That's what this book is about, but keeping secrets is no game.

The board game presents various disaster scenarios such as being attacked by a shark, jumping from a moving train, or being caught in quicksand or in a python's grip…you know, everyday possibilities. For each scenario, response options are given and players must guess which alternative they would attempt in such a dire emergency.

Our personal favorite, because we love Disney's Tower of Terror, is how to survive a plummeting elevator. In both cases, you find yourself in free-fall. Do you jump right before you hit? Do you lie on the floor, or do you just freeze? You'll have to get the game to find out.

Yet one important scenario is missing in this game, but not in this book: What do you do when your skeleton is exposed? How will you respond when your worst secret is suddenly put on parade? I hope you get cold chills thinking about it! You should.

The reason the game skips this situation is because there are no possible escapes from this disaster. If you get busted, you'll be blasted with no mercy! Turn out the lights, the party's over. Being out-ed is your worst-case scenario!

You can escape a grease fire if you don't panic. You can recover from hydroplaning on the freeway if you know how to respond. But if you fall over the guardrail on top of the Empire State Building, you have no option but to enjoy the brief and final adventure. You can't put toothpaste or secrets back in the tube!

What do you do if the video of you and your friend's boyfriend finds its way online (assuming it's a secret)? Your four options might be:

1. Run away;
2. Run away faster;
3. Go into witness protection; or
4. Join the Marines.

When your secrets get out, your options are not really options. They are funeral arrangements. They are tombstone engravings.

That's why you have this book in your hand and not the game of scenarios. We want to help you avoid these situations at all costs! To do so, you'll need the most powerful motivator available: *fear.*

You Need More Than You Have

You are, most likely, already in touch with a chronic sense of dis-ease that your secrets will come out. Unfortunately, our sense of dread can dissipate (just like we stop hearing all those cab horns blowing at night after living in New York City for a time). It's also possible that we grow a bit numb from the nagging sense of dread that occasionally washes over us when our skeletons rattle in our closet and remind us of their risk.

What you must understand is that the absence of significant fear is an open invitation to a serious closet malfunction.

We have a warning for you: *No matter how much fear you carry, it's not enough to keep your secrets safe. A little fear is a dangerous thing. You need enough of that pure energy to maintain a powerful perimeter around your closet. You need enough of that adrenaline to keep you on your toes…or else.*

Imagine the Green Zone in an occupied territory like Afghanistan. This safety area is surrounded by multiple barriers: stone walls, fences, barbed wire, concrete barriers, armed military, surveillance cameras, and layer after layer of emergency preparation. These areas are so well guarded because the threat surrounding them is so real and powerful. This is the mentality of fear you must bring to skeleton security.

Melissa joined the Marines because she knew she needed a challenge. When she came home for a visit after boot camp, her father asked what she had learned in the service so far. The novice Marine said, "Among other things, I learned what the word 'NOW' means."

You need to learn the same thing, especially if you don't wear the uniform. Now is the time to develop a healthy fear that your closet door will slip open and your skeletons will escape. Now is the time to imagine the worst.

Beyond Reactivity

Don't try to be a hero with your secrets! Don't think you can sleepwalk through your week and then suddenly step up and keep the worst from happening. Reacting in the moment is not a strategy, and usually turns out like this…

An older man came strolling up to the Pearly Gates and saw St. Peter waiting. Soon, the saint was going through a book that chronicled the entire history of the man's life.

"Says here you were quite the basketball fan. You went to the tournament even though there was a tornado warning."

"I forgot about that," the man said.

"Says that you stayed home from church if it was sprinkling."

"I'm sure that's not right," the man gulped.

St. Peter began flipping pages, nodding, shaking his head and sighing. Finally, he looked up at the man and asked, "Did you ever do anything exceptional for someone else?"

The man thought for a moment and then said to St. Peter, "Well, I came out of a store and a gang of bikers was taunting this lady. They wanted some money and had her surrounded. To distract them, I started knocking over their motorcycles and using my cane to crack their headlights."

St. Peter looked up from his book for a moment with his eyebrows raised, then scanned through more pages and said, "When did you ever do that?"

"Hmm," the old man said. "I'd say about 10 minutes ago."

Reactivity will never be good enough to protect your skeletons. If you think the fear of an immediate threat is enough, you're an exposure waiting to happen. You need to be proactively afraid. You need to get out in front of your fear and let your fear stay out in front of you.

Do this by employing the threefold strategy of Leanne Kallal. First, she says we should use fear as an important opportunity for self-discovery and self-growth. Second, fear can take us deep into the well of untapped personal power and strength. Third, fear can move us from wishing and wanting to doing and being. We cannot overemphasize this last point enough. Fear moves you beyond wishing your skeletons were gone to making sure they stay buried. Remember to use positive fear talk to undergird these approaches!

Famous Last Words

We suffer from a depletion of fear because we are too naturally blind to what we don't expect and have never considered. History is filled with the infamous last words of people who thought they understood the situation, but did not. They thought they had a handle on life, but they were just fondling their assumptions. Their confidence was not only misplaced, it was *misunderestimated* (to quote a term used by a former President).

These people were not necessarily hiding secrets, but they needed a good dose of fervent fear nevertheless. They fooled themselves into a fool's sense of ease. They went to sleep in the lookout tower. We can see their carelessness now, but they were completely blind to the possibilities at the time. It's hard to imagine how far from reality they were living.

Sensible and Responsible women do not want to vote—infamous words from President Grover Cleveland, who should have feared his senseless and irresponsible wife.

Heavier than air flying machines are impossible—spoken by Lord Kelvin, who lost a fortune in his hot air balloon company.

How cold could it get in Russia?—a question posed by Napoleon, who found out the hard way.

Guitar groups are on their way out—a regrettable decision by Mike Smith of Decca Records when he turned down an opportunity to sign the British rock band called The Beatles.

This overconfidence in one's beliefs and the consequent blindness that ensues is more common than we realize. Whether the belief is about immunity from discovery or something else, it is the beginning of the end. Secret keepers must realize that arrogance about the security of their closets is the ultimate oversight—one that springs from the lack of vigorous fear. You don't want your famously regretted words enshrined on some monument, but that's what could happen if you are casual about what's in your closet!

What do famous last words about secrets sound like? Here are some we have heard. Use your fear to stay far, far away from them.

I thought I could tell my best friend.
It happened so long ago. I thought it would stay buried.
How did he figure out the password to my computer?

I was certain that I had used my other phone.
I know I threw that receipt away.
She's never looked at the credit card bill in the past.

Fear is Freedom

A healthy dose of fear will protect you from such careless exposure. Being afraid of secrets is far better than being afraid to go out in public because you have become another member of the "discredited identity" club. For those not familiar with the formal phrase in quotes, it describes a stigmatized reputation. You don't have to be a sociologist to know how much that sucks.

When it comes to skeleton security, being free of fear is not in the cards if your goal is to keep your secrets safe and locked away. Fear is an essential energy for your success if you want to avoid the maltreatment or ostracism that goes along with being out-ed. That's why we say that fear is actually the door to freedom. When you are open to the motivational power of fear, you are free to pursue your persona.

With apologies to FDR, when it comes to those dark corners of your life, you have nothing to fear but the lack thereof. If you need a bumper sticker to remind you, how about: *Lazy is Crazy!* Laissez -faire security will put you in the sewer of regret more often than "Globe" puts aliens on their cover.

Sure, some people can spin their dirty laundry into reality shows, tabloid attention, and very nice paychecks. These people generate skeletons faster than Apple spits out iPhones. It's nice work if you can get it. The public loves a good zoo, especially

> You won't become a celebrity if your secrets come out. Your persona will become persona non grata.

when the wild animals are celebrities getting busted, fighting paparazzi, or sleeping around.

But this over-exposure doesn't work for most people. You won't become a celebrity if your secrets come out. Your persona will become persona non grata. You'll have all the headaches without the royalties and you'll find yourself cowering in your condo, afraid to be in public.

You see, the choice is not between fear and no fear. Your choice is between fear that motivates you to keep your skeletons secure and fear that paralyzes you due to public humiliation. The difference between the two is vast, as many have discovered.

Leslie could have used a powerful dose of the good fear. Hers was an indiscretion of typical proportions, as she had labeled it in her mind. She had relegated her choice to a minor issue and her mind had shuffled it down into the basement where she never had to imagine what exposure would look and feel like. She came from a very visible family in her religious community, so she was accustomed to getting the benefit of the doubt.

The exotic dancing venture was just a necessary step to secure some capital. She needed a car and wasn't the fast-food type, nor were her parents inclined to spoil her with such a gift. She was away at college and in a big city, so the risks of being discovered seemed minimal, especially since everyone looks different without clothes on. And she thought she looked pretty good. This was confirmed by her popularity. Anyway, she only danced for a year.

Leslie's lack of appropriate fear, two years after the fact, kept her unaware of the negative possibilities. She thought she had taken sufficient steps to distance herself from that former world. Everyone in college goes to parties and everyone posts pictures taken there. Leslie went with some friends to a pretty tame post-game party, as college socials go. Everyone stayed fully dressed and Leslie saw no reason not to post the party pictures she collected of herself and her friends.

But in one of the pictures of Leslie, taken by a friend, she had slipped into a familiar but forgotten sultry pose. She thought it was a cute picture and her mind kept her from making the connection. Without any sense of concern, it was uploaded into permanent cyberspace along with several other shots that were completely ordinary.

She was wakened too early the next day by a friend who wanted to know if she had seen what was on her FB page. "Some creep is like stalking you," she said. "He thinks you're some girl he knows from a dance club. You need to do something fast. He's already posted some pictures of a stripper on his site that looks like you."

Fear would have saved Leslie a great deal of pain and panic. She had set aside her fear of being exposed, thinking of it like a pain-in-the-ass friend. She just ignored the threat. But if you live in la-la-land, your history will find you, not like a pesky friend but like a tidal wave. It will sweep away everything you hold dear about your reputation leaving massive wreckage in its wake.

Leslie tried using the Photoshop strategy to introduce doubt about what was becoming a scandal in her life: "Those pictures of the stripper have been made to look like me; I don't know who that creep is." Sadly, there wasn't enough doubt available, just like there wasn't enough fear in her life to protect her secret.

To help you get that initial infusion of fear that will supercharge your defensive security strategies, try these actionable steps.

1. Channel Your Fear

Fear is always a "pay me now or pay me later" reality, with the latter being more expensive than you want to know. You can either use fear to pay for security, or you can be swallowed up by a more pervasive fear when you fail. One way to get in touch with the fear that motivates is to channel the fear that debilitates.

Think of the scariest movie you've ever seen. Now think of the most frightening scene. Was it a woman moving down a dark hallway or running through the woods? Was it some zombie or alien appearing out of nowhere to consume the hero? Actually, those are sudden frights that don't do justice to the constant and repressive fear that comes when you've been out-ed.

A better scene would be that of James Franco's character in the movie 127 Hours, a rock climber, stuck for days and running out of time because his arm is wedged between two rocks and he cannot get it free. At last, in utter desperation (and disgust), he breaks his own bones and cuts the arm off with a dull knife.

Sure it's terrifying, but that's the image you need to remember when you're stuck between the persona you have worked so hard to develop, and the new one you'll be stuck with when your crazy skeleton goes running loose in the streets.

It takes fear to avoid the terror that will visit you if your secrets come out in IMAX 3D! Then, while your skeletons are having a pride parade, you'll be stuck hiding in the same closet where they should have been locked away! That's irony you can live without.

When your skeletons come out, your reputation becomes another victim of the Texas Chainsaw Massacre. When your secrets become grapevine gossip, you'll find out what they really mean by 'night of the living dead.'

Being exposed is not like movie fright that passes quickly with a nervous laugh and another trip to the concession area. The terror of exposure gives you permanent nightmares; the ones that keep showing up like that stray cat you fed once.

Why not channel your moments of terror in the theater or elsewhere to jumpstart your motivational drive? Imagining your own secrets on the big screen and your friends and family in the audience should send the right kind of chills down your spine.

2. Log On To Fear

If you have an internal dial for fear, turn it up when you're on social media. Avoid these famous last words, "I thought my information was private." The road to an admirable and advantageous persona is strewn with the wreckage of random pictures and impulsive tweets. Remember the old adage: if it seems like a good idea at the time, it probably isn't.

We deal with appropriate ways to use social media for skeleton maintenance in other chapters, but the first principle of being online is always fear. Make it part of your start-up menu, so fear boots up just like Safari. Memories of words, images, and experiences fade and distort over time, but data on servers will live and rattle around forever, or longer. A good dose of paranoia is no picnic to be sure, but it's better than the full frontal assault of public exposure.

Everyone is over-focused on vulnerability to hackers. But hackers are only interested in your financial information. They could care less about your porn or your emails to your secret lover.

The real risk you have online is that you think social media is a personal asset instead of a liability. You think being connected is about finding out what your friends are doing every moment of every day, when the information explosion is really about how much your friends can find out about you.

It doesn't take full exposure to ruin your life. It only takes an inch; a sniff; a glimpse; a whisper; and it's "welcome to the gossip channel." You must believe us. Most people prefer innuendo over evidence; suspicion over substance; a hint over honesty. We think we've just defined social media. Better log on to fear.

The movie Doubt, set in the Bronx in the year 1964, was nominated for 5 Academy awards. The story's two main characters are Father Flynn, a progressive and compassionate priest, and Sister Alouysius, a stern principal of the school who suspects and rejects anything and everything outside her own conviction. She will not allow students, for instance, the use of ballpoint pens because that will lead to the degradation of penmanship. She would really love Twitter.

The sister takes exception to Father Flynn's sermons, his use of sugar in his tea, his use of ballpoint pens, and his gentle ways with students. So when Father Flynn takes a special interest in the school's first black student, Sister Alouysius believes the relationship must be inappropriate.

Whether she is correct is unimportant. Having no real evidence is beside the point. Based upon her own impulses alone, she takes steps to have the priest removed. She is completely right in her own mind, and that's all that matters to her.

And that's all that will matter for some people who are plugged into your online presence. Who knows why they want to see you knocked down a few notches. These people don't have to wear habits because they have the bad habit of accusing first and asking questions never. All they need is a suggestion and most people post those every day! As they say, don't be concerned about yelling. It's the whispers that will kill you.

We are suggesting you employ the same kind of fear in online skeleton security that prompts you to check three times that the stove is off before you leave for vacation. Isn't that better than the torture of wondering if you left it on when you're 200 miles down the road? It's certainly better than coming home to a crispy condo!

You need fear like your body needs protein. Instead of trying to relax, use that fear to your advantage. It will give you the edge you need to stay on top of your skeletons. We want you to remember that old line from an early horror film: "Be afraid. Be very afraid!"

3. Check The Backdoors

Sometimes our closets have backdoors that we create when we aren't sufficiently afraid. We create these "openings" when we are feeling warm and safe and then we forget about them.

A secure closet requires you to revisit old decisions around your secrets to check for vulnerabilities. Let fear be your guide as you do the inventory. Here's a story to show you what can happen when you're not afraid.

Kirsten was dating a real jerk when she got pregnant. "Of course it was unplanned," she screamed at her friend. "Who would plan to have a child with Tom the Player unless they were in a drunken stupor?"

She dumped the loser dad, kept the child, and decided she would be the best mother she could be. During her pregnancy, she met Stuart. They had instant chemistry and soon after Kirsten gave birth to Kyle, she and Stuart were engaged. They had also decided, and it was Stuart's idea, to list him as the father on Kyle's birth certificate. For Kirsten, it felt like the perfectly loving and honorable thing to do; not really a secret that would harm anyone. This was the backdoor she created.

Kirsten discovered the backdoor one Saturday morning, 14 years later, when she was at one of Kyle's soccer games. The two of them were walking to the concession stand when suddenly they were face to face with Kyle's biological father, Tom.

Kirsten had repressed the reality that Kyle looked very much his father, but as they stood right next to each other, the resemblance was breathtaking. While Kirsten was having an internal panic attack, Tom was getting no small amount of pleasure telling Kyle how he and Kirsten had been very good friends back in the old days and what a fine looking young man he was.

All Kirsten remembered, as she tried to run and hide, was Tom calling out, "Looks like maybe we should talk sometime."

There's no need to replay the months of anxiety and discussion that ensued between Kirsten and Stuart. Kyle was obviously sensing that something was amiss, but didn't know how to address it. Therapy sessions followed. Eventually, they told Kyle the truth, which turned his life upside down. As you can imagine, it didn't do much for the marriage either.

Kirsten had an old sleeping skeleton she had put to bed in her mind. "Out of sight" had become "out of mind." Her closet had a backdoor because her new life moved her past an old fear that would have been the edge she needed. Now that it's too late, she has fear in spades. More sad irony.

Before you get out-ed, get out of touch with that naïve sense of immunity that creates other entrances to your closet. Better to be apprehensive than to be apprehended by a calamitous new reality that is completely out of control.

4. Use Imagination Sessions

You must hold onto your fear. When you have boney figures in your closet or basement, you must keep them on your mind or they will start poking around in your life upstairs and outside. You cannot have that intrusion into your public life and persona.

As part of your Pretense Plan, we suggest daily imagination sessions. While it is important to use the left hemisphere of your brain when you are developing a denial plan, the creative capacity of your right hemisphere is more effective for imagination and pretense. We hope you're impressed by our total brain approach to skeleton security.

For imagination exercises, we suggest setting aside some time when you're already worried about something. No sense starting from scratch. Simply close your eyes, unless you're operating heavy machinery, and imagine a fear-inducing scenario, such as being at a party filled with all the people you know and love.

Imagine that the host stops the music, grabs a microphone and asks for everyone's attention. As a hush falls over the crowd, the host motions to you and asks you to step up on the stage. With every eye watching, she smiles and says, "I have just been told the juiciest story of the year. You aren't going to believe this."

Now imagine that the host gestures toward you and says, "I've just learned that (put your name and secret here)!" Imagine the responses of your friends, or former friends. Picture them as they choke on their Pinot Grigio. Imagine someone in your family running from the room. Everyone's mouth is open and the laughter begins. Feel the blood rushing to your face and your heart pounding out of your chest as you look for the closest exit or cyanide capsule.

And finally, imagine that there are no exit doors; that you are frozen on stage as partygoers point and cackle. Get a good picture of that scene because once people get a look into your closet, that's what they will be doing.

That's just one example. Your imagination is a deep source of these terrifying scenarios. You can come up with others. Use them to amp up your fear.

Your Fear Factor

Just one person can turn your Mayberry Peace into the Amityville Horror. That's why fear can be so helpful and why it's so accessible. We suggest testing your fear level on a regular basis to guard against apathetic exposure.

A first grade teacher was doing a lesson on home safety and had brought some "show and tell" objects from home as props. She reached into her sack of surprises and pulled out a battery-powered smoke alarm. Then she pushed the test button and the familiar high-pitched sound followed, along with squeals and children covering their ears.

"What does it mean when you hear that sound," the teacher asked the class?

Johnny's hand went up first and he was called upon. "It means daddy's cooking supper," he said.

Test your fear more often than you test your smoke alarms. Feel what being busted would be like and bottle that emotion. Then distill it into 100-proof security that will make your closet the next Fort Knox.

Use this checklist to test the strength of your fear. Is your skeleton fear competitive with the best phobias in the world? How do you measure up? Indicate how much fear is fueling your security by assigning a score of 1-10 for each statement. 1 means you completely disagree and 10 is a perfect score. The more points you get, the better your fear factor.

1. I get sweaty palms every time I think about what's in my closet.
2. I'd rather be overrun by spiders in my bed than locked in the closet with my skeletons.
3. Counting terrorists at night helps me fall asleep while counting my secrets is certain insomnia.
4. Being publicly rejected by a lover is child's play compared to having my skeleton exposed.
5. I'd rather stutter and stammer my way through a thousand public speeches than be embarrassed about my secret self.
6. Even though heights make me weak in the knees and light in the head, I'd rather walk a support beam on a skyscraper than witness my skeletons running free.
7. Failure at business, sport, or relationship is not a problem if I don't have a failure of the deadbolt on my closet.
8. Nuclear attack? It's quick and painless compared to the slow death of deception discovery.
9. Death is not the problem. A slow death by embarrassment is.

We all remember how presidential candidate John Edwards created a love child with his mistress. It was crazy enough that he had a mistress on the campaign trail in the first place. It was beyond crazy that he made a sex tape of one of their encounters. But then came the pregnancy, which was another nail in the coffin. Edwards had to manage some campaign money to take care of the mistress and child, and then talked an associate into claiming that he, not Edwards, was the father. This is a classic case of the invincibility infection that causes a shortage of fear. It will ruin you.

Closet failure from lack of fear can be avoided if you stay committed. Fear your exposure like the CIA fears intelligence failures. Fear it like a pharmaceutical company fears massive side effects for its wonder drug.

At AA, they fake it 'till they make it. Our motto is, "Fear it, or they'll smear it." "Be afraid. Be very afraid."

Chapter Five

Plausible Deniability

Non-attribution to the United States for covert operations was the original and principal purpose of the so-called doctrine of "plausible denial."
—United States Senate Select Committee
to Study Governmental Operations

Now that you are dressed for diversion, learning from the masters, going on the offensive, and pumped up with that super motivator called fear, we want to challenge you to step up your intelligence game. It has been said that "military intelligence" is an oxymoron, and "emotional intelligence" a key business asset. What we say is that "closet intelligence" is your best personal asset.

You are five chapters into a process of developing a higher CIQ (closet intelligence quotient). We want to build on that momentum by teaching you some of the best diversionary tactics ever developed. They are elite strategies because they were developed for the dark and dangerous world of international espionage.

As former Vice-President Al Gore has noted, the truth is often inconvenient. We have found this to be especially relevant when that truth is scandalous and taking up significant space in your closet. You don't have the luxury of forgetting where you've shortchanged your values. That's why you need a super-intelligent Skeleton Code strategy of historic proportions called *Plausible Deniability*.

President Truman, in 1948, defined covert operations as "...all activities conducted pursuant to this directive which are so planned and executed that any U.S. Government responsibility for them is not evident to unauthorized persons and that if uncovered the U.S. Government can plausibly disclaim any responsibility for them." The CIA then coined the phrase, 'Plausible Deniability.'

Those of us who grew up watching the TV series *Mission Impossible* remember the message that was delivered to Mr. Phelps each week. After describing the covert mission, and before the recording incinerated, the voice on the tape said "remember, should you or any of your IM force be caught our killed, the Secretary will disavow any knowledge of your action."

Plausible Deniability has been used effectively on a global scale for decades. It's genius, really, and not just applicable to spies, governments, and reality television stars. This is a tactic you can use at home. It works for your personal covert operations. Why should the CIA have all the good toys and tools? If it's good enough for Langley, it's good enough for us. We do not recommend skirting the law, however, though it is common for intelligence agencies. You don't have to keep it true, but you should keep it legal. This will limit your effectiveness only slightly and will keep your closet from getting too crowded.

Develop a Deniability Plan

In our examination of how to keep secrets, we've found that denial is the best river in Egypt or anywhere else. But not just any type of denial will do. Ask the president who famously said, "I did not have sex with that woman," or the coach who said, "I didn't know my players were being entertained by strippers," or the long list of athletes who said, "I did not use performance enhancing drugs."

Denial in the face of hard evidence or media frenzy is nothing but a desperate curtain call. It's a remedy that will kill you before the disease has a chance. Desperate disavowal will only dig you deeper into disaster.

One of the most viewed videos ever to be seen on YouTube was the final play of the 2007 game between Trinity University and Millsaps College. It was very much like the final play of the 2015 Miami-Duke football game. Trinity was behind with two seconds left on the clock. They were 61 yards away from the goal line. Everyone in the stadium expected a Hail Mary pass, but instead, the quarterback hit a receiver 15 yards over the middle.

The defense converged on him and he tossed the ball back to another player, who ran until he was about to be tackled and then tossed the ball to another player.

This play didn't come out of any playbook. You couldn't draw it out with X's and O's if you wanted to. You have to see it to believe it, but the runners went from one side of the field to the other looking for daylight. The play lasted for over a minute and ended after 15 laterals and a winning touchdown by Trinity.

This desperate play was watched by so many because dumb luck works less often than winning the lottery. It was a fluke of nature and when it comes to denial, you don't want to depend on a fluke.

You need something better than reactive denial, especially the kind that is delivered as a frantic defense. Whether you have retired (old) secrets or active skeletons in your closet, it is important that you create some plausible cushion between your public persona and your closet self. Remember, the keyword is "plausible." You don't have to reach such heights as "verifiable or demonstrable."

We suggest developing a formal Deniability Plan or Pretense Plan using our skeleton guidelines. This plan will be as valuable to you as the inflatable slide on the emergency exit of a passenger jet, or the designated driver that took you home after that fraternity party.

A great Deniability Plan will always have certain strengths. Here and only here, we are providing you with our Elite Eight strategies to develop plausible denials. Please plan and practice all of them. Using your best CIQ, devise:

1. Several quick responses that vary based on the circumstances.
Great denial never looks like the squirrel frozen by fear in the middle of the road. Silence and/or stammering answers are dead giveaways. Just like having jumper cables in your trunk or Kleenex in your purse, have some ready responses in your head when your closet door is breached. This requires forward thinking.

Some people find these verbal escape routes easy and natural to access, like Justin, a high school student working in the produce section of a grocery store. One day, an older and rather eccentric woman approached him in the fruit section and said she wanted to buy half a cantaloupe.

"I don't think we sell them by halves," he said in disbelief while trying to be polite.

"Well go ask your manager," she snipped.

So Justin, seeing the manager standing nearby, approached him and said, "You won't believe this, but a crazy woman over there behind me wants to buy half a cantaloupe."

And as he was saying this, the manager's face changed into something sheepish, and Justin heard an "Ahem" behind him, coming from the woman in question.

He turned to see her standing there with arms crossed and said to the manager, "And this lovely lady wants to buy the other half."

Later, the manager found Justin and said, "That was some very quick thinking on your part...a nice recovery. Where did you learn to do that?"

"Oh, in Minnesota, where I grew up." He said. "All we have up there are crazy women and hockey players."

"My wife is from Minnesota," the manager frowned.

"Wow," said the young man. "Which hockey team did she play for?"

Unfortunately, most of us don't have that much CIQ and can't find such convenient escapes when we need them. But all of us can plan ahead and have the right reply for our most likely vulnerabilities.

Don't try to be plausible on the fly. Diversions don't typically drop out of the sky. What usually happens is that we think of what we could have said an hour later, which is much too late. You need several plausible denials planned well ahead of time; alternatives to your secret that put you at least one step removed from the disturbing exposure. It's ok to be a little OCD when it comes to keeping several of these sharp arrows in your closet quiver. Rehearse delivering the lines while you're in the shower.

A great Deniability Plan should also include:

2. An appeal to some familiar source of carelessness or confusion.

The big three credit rating bodies are known for screwing up information and mixing up identities. It's practically impossible to get them to correct their mistakes, and they have made life miserable for thousands of consumers. When you develop a deniability story that includes an organization like this, it will immediately create sympathy and understanding by others.

Many, for instance, have blamed Photoshop or some other editing software when their exposures have been image-based. You may even be lucky enough to have a friend who was once misidentified or accused. Hacking is as widespread as identity theft. Never hesitate to drop names and experiences. Most people don't want to pile on victims who are part of an oppressed group.

Brad's deniability plan included an admission of getting into trouble with the law as a means of maintaining his greater secret of actual prison time. He knew people would be eager to believe his story about the cop who pressured him into a confession, while his only mistake had been hanging out with the wrong people at the wrong time. Every time another prisoner is in the news, being exonerated by DNA evidence, Brad rests a little easier knowing that it makes his story all the more plausible.

Remember: the goal is to appeal to some familiar sense of carelessness or confusion, especially when that association can connect with the other person's empathetic capacities.

A third ingredient of great deniability is:

3. Specificity that is uncomplicated.

Con artists are known for their elaborate stories designed to act like mental mazes—plotlines so complex you can't really follow or trace them. These aggressive actors overwhelm you with information that then becomes like mental quicksand. It only works on the timid and naïve. People telling complex stories might as well be screaming, "Look what a great liar I am."

A plausible story, on the other hand, is short, succinct, and specific. It is unencumbered by details, which also makes it easier to use under pressure.

Sam grows a few cannabis plants in the back of his residential property, which runs up against an adjacent cemetery. He also knows of some kids with attitude down the street that he keeps an eye on. If his plants are discovered, he will simply put two and two together. He will shake his head and with frustration say, "I'm sorry I don't keep that area back there mowed down like I should, but now you've helped me understand why I've see those boys hanging around behind my place at the edge of the cemetery so much."

Notice that Sam doesn't protest or simply pretend to be ignorant. He connects some simple dots in a way that is succinct and plausible. If he keeps his place clear of evidence, he can also invite the police inside to check things out, reminding them that he will help any way he can.

Keep your denial simple and straightforward, free of details you might forget later on. Remember, the goal is not to create a complex sense of certainty, but to be plausible without raising additional questions.

This fourth strategy is very important to your Plan. Make sure you have:

4. At least one truth that is easily verifiable.

Our intelligence services do this so well. When they want to put an operative into foreign territory, that resource doesn't just have false credentials to pose as a health worker or teacher. They actually have the expertise, along with the espionage training, of course. When they are checked, they really do have the knowledge that supports their identity.

Liz didn't like alcohol, but did find the occasional recreational use of painkillers enjoyable, especially when her work was intense. She figured she was too fearful of addiction to overuse them. Even so, she didn't want her husband to know about it.

So each time she obtained a new supply for her chronic knee pain, she put them in an old bottle that dated back to the kidney stone she passed; conveniently, the prescription that introduced her to the oxycodone family in the first place. This allowed her to stash the bottle in the most remote corner of the under-sink cabinet, which was a place out of the way but completely plausible if discovered.

If the bottle was noticed, she could simply say, "Oh that must be from the time I had my kidney stone. Let me see the bottle. Yeah, that's the date I'd rather not remember. I think I kept them in case I had another. They say that's likely if you've ever had one."

As any good defense attorney knows, you don't have to overwhelm the jury with evidence in order to create "reasonable doubt." When it comes to plausible deniability, all you need is one bit of solid evidence that is consistent with your story, especially when you are under pressure.

When your closet door is cracked, don't think you can dazzle the curious with BS and expect them to appreciate the aroma. One good piece of evidence in your favor will be enough.

You may think this next idea will backfire, but it is highly effective. Make sure your denial includes:

5. A reference to some minor confession.

Rather than attempting to present yourself as the latest incarnation of Captain Kangaroo or Mr. Rogers, throw in some controlled candor if your skeleton is at risk. Don't try to be above all suspicion. Just be above the worst of it. Give 'em a bone.

As you are denying, admit to something secondary or superfluous, such as 'hanging out with the wrong person' one time, or some other universal weakness. This will satisfy your inquisitor's taste for triumph.

They will conclude that they were right in their intuitive suspicions, but off target a bit. Give them a lesser target and everyone walks away satisfied. They managed to get their piece of flesh and you managed to relock your closet.

A poor excuse is often worse than none at all, so be prepared. This is one place you don't need to mimic political masters. When confronted with their skeletons, they have only one move: they dig in their heels. They believe if they deny the charges often enough and passionately enough, we will start to believe them. But their digging just buries them deeper, as their denial invites more scrutiny.

Business leaders are a little better at this strategy of partial confession. For instance, Enron's Jeffrey Skilling, under the glare for serious corporate malfeasance that destroyed thousands of people's retirements, said, "I am devastated by and apologetic about what Enron has come to represent."

It's almost virtuous to express this kind of "apology." Skilling was reminding everyone how committed he was to Enron and how serious he took their image. At the same time, he was making the quintessential business apology: that stockholders had lost value. While his form was good, we should mention for purposes of full disclosure that he was convicted of 19 counts of securities fraud and other charges. Most closets can't withstand this level of investigation.

Better to admit to some minor failure before your closet bottom falls out. "Yes, I did lose some money in the office pool trying to win that huge lottery prize," is better than, "I'm still losing $100 a week playing the slots." Remember, this strategy shifts the attention away from what you're really hiding.

Another expression of a high Closet Intelligence Quotient is the ability to plan:

6. A strategy that achieves impact more than information.

Staying the night where you shouldn't be? Don't plan an informational strategy. Aim for the heart. Simply park on the street and raise your hood. One never knows when a car will give out, and pity covers more suspicion than rationale. Remember to include how difficult it was to break down like that.

When you are planning your denial, consider the words of Joseph Goebbels: "We don't speak to communicate anything, but to create a certain effect." What you say is not as important as its ability to calm, reassure, or create confidence. You must feign concern or in some way identify with the interrogator's issue.

We suggest you play the role of a therapist or philosopher for this strategy. Memorize some of these phrases to have on hand when the time is right. Use them to create a sense of connection with the person who may be sniffing around your closet. Often they will shift the attention 180 degrees.

"I'm hearing some pain in your voice. Is there anything I can do?"

"I'm sorry this is causing you pain or agitation. Tell me how you're feeling."

"I hope you're being kind to yourself and taking care of yourself."

"If you need to talk about this, you know I'm willing to listen."

"You know I love you even when you're upset."

"When you're not feeling just right, it's time for ice-cream."

"I really love it when you're all about keeping it real."

As therapists realize, when someone gets critical of you or seeks to blame you, they are dealing with their own guilt and pain by projecting it onto you. They really need therapy and you can give them the next best thing: an empathetic and listening ear that makes them feel like they have been understood, even if they are a closet case.

These prying people may think they are looking for information, but they aren't. They are looking for a feeling that they are OK; a sense that they are better than others; an emotional equilibrium that they have lost.

When you give them a taste of empathy or concern, they will quickly loose interest in your closet. Your denial goal is emotional impact, not information.

The seventh characteristic of a great denial plan is:

7. A liberal and disarming use of humor.

There's nothing that walks more like guilt and quacks more like guilt than anger, bravado, or emotional collapse. When people have nothing to hide, they don't turn into the Tasmanian devil or curl up in the fetal position. They find some humor in any situation.

Therapist and systems consultant Ed Friedman famously understood that seriousness was a universal symptom of anxiety. People who hide skeletons are chronically and naturally anxious about being out-ed, and are therefore some of the most serious people on the planet. Seriousness, therefore, invites suspicion. In fact, it screams suspicion.

Therefore, humor becomes an essential ingredient in your deniability plan. You must project ease with yourself and others rather than taking yourself too seriously.

Mark Twain and other humorists are excellent sources for quips and quotes you can memorize and dispense when necessary. Humor has a powerfully distracting and sedating effect on people. Use it when you can. It is one denial strategy that is difficult to overuse.

Humor is especially effective if it can be self-deprecating. If your closet has a crack and someone is too curious, drop your drawers (figuratively of course) and make them laugh. Here are some classic areas about which we can all poke fun at ourselves. Laughter is a powerful diversion.

- Your physical build
- Some physical feature like baldness or a big nose
- Being nerdish or otherwise socially awkward
- Being forgetful
- The way you dress
- The car you drive or the way you get around
- Your name or nickname
- How you waste your money
- Your most embarrassing experience
- Something quirky about yourself

Humor is actually an effective way to accomplish goal #6, which is to make an emotional impact, but it deserves to be treated as a separate strategy. Nothing lowers suspicion and elevates a sense of wellbeing like humor. Use it more than your momma used butter when she baked a cake.

The last characteristic of an Elite Eight denial plan is that it will:

8. Cover all contingencies.

Your plan for plausible doubt should contain what we call skeletal contingencies. You might want to call them back-up plans. Every great team and every great movement has them.

W.C. Fields, an infamous agnostic, was once caught in his dressing room reading a Bible. Embarrassed and not wanting to be mis-understood, Fields snapped the book shut and explained, "I was just looking for loopholes."

A great deniability plan will consider all contingencies. It will consider all potential exits and options, so that your denial will move as smoothly as Fred Astaire and Ginger Rogers covered the dance floor.

Look for loopholes in your cover stories like you look for bargains at the mall. Turn them over and inspect them like you would a fresh peach at the market. When you discover a good one, list it in a highly secure and

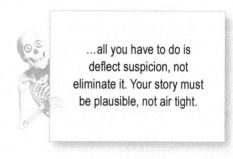

...all you have to do is deflect suspicion, not eliminate it. Your story must be plausible, not air tight.

confidential place without labeling it as such.

Some people collect recipes so that they are always prepared to whip up a good meal. We recommend collecting and keeping a sensible list of cover stories appropriate for what's in your closet. Remember, all you have to do is deflect suspicion, not eliminate it. Your story must be plausible, not air tight. Imagine being your own defense attorney. Reasonable doubt is a sufficient standard.

Marvin had a deniability plan. It was simple and ingenious. He simply told his wife that the laptop he purchased was used, even though it was not. He told her that he found the computer online and bought it from a guy who wanted to upgrade. He made a big deal out of this, lest his wife ignore him in the usual way.

Now, if the rather straight-laced wife ever finds porn on Marvin's computer, he has a plan. He is prepared to feign shock and then lay the problem at the feet of that guy who sold him the computer. He will even apologize for not taking it to the computer store to make sure it was wiped clean, a step he will take right away, along with coming up with a better password.

Had Marvin not created a plan and set it up to perfection, he would be in deep doo-doo, as well as in counseling with his wife, which for him was redundant. Had he been caught unprepared, he would have fumbled and stumbled and probably confessed. Then he would never have heard the end of it.

But Marvin won't have to bother with therapy because he considered the contingencies and had a strategy that was prepared and plausible. And his wife obviously wanted to believe it and get back to her daytime television.

Use your imagination when devising contingency plans. You'll be amazed at what pops into your mind.

Spurious Strategies

Being unprepared to address a security breach is simply not an option. Stammering and stuttering in response to a leak is tantamount to a confession. Stories made up on the spot are very risky and usually unconvincing. She's not going to believe that aliens hacked your computer and uploaded porn. A bad explanation only serves as an invitation to poke around more.

We conclude this chapter with a warning about techniques that are ineffective. They may be natural reactions to exposure or may otherwise seem appropriate, but they have significant failure rates.

1. Hurt and Outrage

We have heard it suggested that expressing hurt or outrage is an appropriate and effective response to skeleton exposure, but we strongly disagree. We've heard too many stories.

Karen left her phone out and it was not password protected. So her curious and jealous boyfriend, Brian, picked it up for a look. There he found some very flirtatious text messages to one of Karen's old boyfriends—a guy she no longer had any contact with, so she said.

When she came downstairs, Brian had the phone in his hand with the texts showing on the screen. Karen, predictably, flew into a rage: "How dare you look at my phone, etc., etc." After some good angry argument, that started with the old boyfriend and included her spending habits and other irritations, Karen tried shifting to the "I'm hurt" strategy. It didn't work on Brian, and it probably won't work on the person who stumbles upon your secret.

No, we don't think protesting too much or pretending to be hurt is a good plan if you're serious about your skeletons. The keyword for your plan is "plausible" not "passionate."

2. Too Self-Centered

Those who want to discover our secrets and bring us down are often on a quest to elevate their own sense of superiority. If we attempt diversions that seem self-serving, we will merely fuel their fire. Avoid denials that exhibit pride.

Sandy was active in her church, but she had a pretty wild side in college. Occasionally, she still liked to do a little "coke" for old times sake. When she drove across town to a supplier, she was always afraid someone would spot her car and inquire what brought her to the area.

So Sandy came up with a plausible diversion. If anyone asked, she'd say, "I was delivering some care packages I helped put together for shipment to poor people in Haiti."

She could have said, "Mind your own business," but this would invite more investigation. Instead, she chose the path of humility. Anytime you can include charity in your diversion, you will increase your chances of security by 50%!

When using a denial plan, stay clear of anything that smells like arrogance.

3. Running Out of Ideas

There is a T-shirt that says, "I'm cleverly disguised as a responsible adult." People may buy T-shirts like that, but they don't buy the slogans printed on them. You need ideas that are more convincing, and you'll have to use your best CIQ to put them into practice.

When the power goes out after a storm, you will need a good supply of food and water. You also need a decent stockpile of plausible denials for your closet. One good denial won't take you the distance in skeleton security.

Early in his career, P.T. Barnum, of circus fame, created an exhibit entitled "The Happy Family." It was a cage consisting of a lion, a tiger, a panther, and a young lamb. Attendance at his shows soared as people flocked to see this amazing spectacle. No one could imagine a lamb co-existing with such predators.

Some time later, a reporter asked Barnum about his future plans for the Happy Family. Off the record, he said, "It will become a permanent display, if the supply of lambs holds out."

The moral of the story: keep a good supply of cover stories that keep you distant from your secret. As someone said, "good cover stories are like a string of pearls…lovely, smooth, and worth every penny."

4. Social Media Sloth

We must make one closing warning about social media. Our information often seems safe and anonymous online, but that is far from reality.

Scholars like Robert Feldman believe that Americans are becoming more dishonest by creating a "culture of deception" in social media. Clearly, lying on social websites is much easier than in person, and this is doubly true if your identity remains anonymous.

But be careful. Anonymity is an illusion. When your deceptions go digital, they go permanent and public. You'll never be able to shove them in a closet. You'll never find a lock that will hold.

Secrets and social media can create feeding frenzies. When you mix them, they can take on an uncontrollable life of their own. Ask former Congressman Anthony Weiner, former NBA owner Donald Sterling, or former Pennsylvania Supreme Court Justice Seamus McCaffery. Note the common denominator in this list: *Former.*

The bottom line is this: Posting can get you into a world of trouble but is never sufficient to get you out. You will need plans that are independent of your online presence.

Let's Recap

Plausible deniability is effective at the highest levels of government and can also be used to guard your lowly closet. We have challenged you to prepare for exposure risks by using our Elite Eight strategies for plausibility.

1. Have a quiver full of quick responses;
2. Connect your denial to a familiar source of confusion;
3. Use only a touch of specificity and avoid complicated arguments;
4. Make sure your denial has at least one verifiable element of truth;
5. Include a minor confession in your denial that satisfies and secures;
6. Devise a denial that majors on emotional impact over information;
7. Use humor to de-escalate and self-deprecate;
8. Consider all your vulnerabilities and create contingencies for each.

Plausible deniability has been most often used to protect high-ranking officials from actions carried out on their behalf by lower-ranking officials. What a perfect rationale for its use in secret keeping. Your public persona is the one with higher rank and your secret self is that low-ranking rascal doing what your persona cannot officially sanction.

Denials are great options to keep in your toolbox. Just be sure to make them passably plausible!

Chapter Six

One Way Trust

Never trust anything that can think for itself
if you can't see where it keeps its brain.
—J.K. Rowling

If you are implementing the secret strategies we have outlined in this book so far, then your skeletons are in a much safer place. Each additional strategy you put into play will have a multiplying effect on your overall security, so keep going.

Who among us has not turned the wrong way on a one-way street, usually in an unfamiliar city? When you get yourself turned around in traffic, you know how quickly you can get into serious trouble. In this chapter, we are going to help you navigate the one-way street called "trust," so you don't create a personal pileup that will ruin more than just your day.

Put very simply, we are going to help you make sure your trust is always moving in the right direction, meaning people will trust you, but you will not trust them. The right direction is from other people to you and never the other way around.

Ms. Rowling is correct. You just never know where people keep their brains, though we have our suspicions. While we could suggest, with some confidence, where most men keep theirs, we prefer to take the high road.

What you can be sure of is that there are people in your life who like to keep their attention focused on other people: what they do; who they like; where they go; and worst of all, what they're keeping in their closets. We're the same way; always attuned to the scrumptious secrets our friends or coworkers may be hiding.

Don't be fooled: those who act like they're on the high road still love the lowdown. You can never know with certainty which friends may have these intentions, so we have found it best to keep your trust locked up just as safely as your secrets!

Healthy Skepticism

In the game of secrets, naiveté is a "Get Out of Jail Free" card for your skeletons. We have never known a good skeleton keeper who did not also have a healthy, daily dose of skepticism. The problem here is that "trust traffic" isn't marked as clearly as the kind with automobiles.

Sure, we all know a few people that might as well be wearing "Do Not Trust" signs around their necks. As the saying goes, *never trust your secrets to someone nicknamed 'Chug-a-lug.'* But not every trust trap is so clearly marked.

Several years ago, H&R Block offered a chance for one of their customers to win a one million dollar prize. Glen and Gloria Sims of Sewell, New Jersey won the drawing, but did not believe the H&R Block representative who called to tell them the good news. There are so many scammers out there.

The company kept trying to call Glen and Gloria and also sent several letters, but the couple was convinced that it was a practical joke or just more junk mail. They had once responded to the gift of a vacation that turned out to be a daylong infomercial on a timeshare. They weren't going to do that again, so they trashed the notices and hung up on callers.

One last representative phoned to say the deadline for accepting the prize was about to pass and that NBC's Today Show was going to run a story on the couple's refusal to accept $1,000,000. It would have made a good story for TV, but not so good for the fools who passed up the big prize.

At that point, Glen decided to investigate further (good choice) and discovered that he and his wife had actually won the big one. They appeared a few days later on the Today Show to say they had indeed accepted the prize money (good choice) and that their cynicism was somewhat abated.

For every true story that ends well like this, there are one million that end badly for people who trust too easily and quickly.

We think "you can't be too careful" is a good standard to follow. Glen and Gloria are shining examples of the skepticism you need to nurture when it comes to guarding your skeletons. Your friends and neighbors are scam artists when it comes to secrets. They will tell you anything to get their foot in the door of your closet, just like marketers. They do this to avoid getting near their own skeleton hiding grounds. If a daily aspirin is good for a heart patient, then take at least two doses of skepticism.

One helpful and easy exercise to increase your capacity for skepticism and suspicion is what we call "TV Talkback." Whenever a commercial comes on, simply engage the message as if another person were speaking to you. Remember to use a loud and emphatic voice.

When the actor says that a reverse mortgage is a great way to get out of your debts, tell them in the strongest language permissible that they are full of _____.

When you learn that you can save $3,000 by purchasing a $40,000 car, laugh out loud and ask them how long they have been mathematically impaired, or something stronger if your household can stand it.

When you are told that a certain perfume or cologne will cause people of the opposite sex to throw themselves at you, stand up, stomp your feet and tell the creators of this marketing where they can stick their message. Be creative.

You get the idea. Make it a game. Soon, you'll develop a pattern of distrusting anything you hear that initially sounds appealing. This capacity will come in handy when you are tempted to trust a friend. When it comes to trust, it's important to start with your foot on the brake. Be a hard sell.

Or Else...

Those who do relationships with a suspicion deficit are heading straight into oncoming traffic. There are no worse collisions than the head-on variety. Take Claris and Rhonda, for instance.

They had developed a really nice friendship over several years, meeting when their children were in the same preschool. As the load of mothering drove them both to the edge of sanity, they found respite in their conversations, texts, and occasional lunches.

As Rhonda's husband climbed the corporate ladder, she was the recipient of nice benefits. Claris was clearly aware of her friend's new financial advantages, and irritated by the lack of her own.

The one thing Claris had that Rhonda did not was a good marriage. Her husband was thoughtful and romantic, shared the parenting and some housework, and was a very good listener. Rhonda, on the other hand, was always talking about how distant and uncaring her husband could be. He was only interested in work and cars and hardly gave her the time of day. There was no intimacy.

When Rhonda told Claris that she had feelings for another man, Claris was not surprised, but she was upset. The object of Rhonda's affection was married to a woman that Claris knew—a woman from a very nice family. When Claris tried to counsel Rhonda away from this fool's errand, she was dismissed as being over-reactive. It was just harmless flirtation. That was all.

Claris knew better. She saw the signs. When Rhonda went to the ladies room one day when they were having lunch, Claris glanced at her phone long enough to see a multitude of texts from the same number. When she read just one of them, she thought the phone might melt in her hand.

At that moment she knew that something needed to be done to stop the train wreck that was coming. Her idea would cause problems for Rhonda in the short term, but would perhaps be the catalyst she needed to address her own marriage.

Claris created a new email address and wrote an anonymous note to the wife of Rhonda's new interest. She simply suggested that the wife would be well served to check her husband's phone records and look at his computer. She did not mention any names.

In less than 48 hours, Rhonda was calling to see if Claris could meet her right away. "Something terrible" had happened.

She was right. The terrible thing that happened was that she trusted a friend with a big secret. She thought it was safe to hide a skeleton in a friend's closet, but she could not have been more mistaken.

Trust is the femme fatale of human relationships. Trust will seduce you like Helen of Troy and create an epic catastrophe. Trust will draw you in like the Sirens and destroy your cover. Trust will lure you into thinking how much you love the femme while she is preparing to suck your secrets out like a vampire.

It's all well and good if people want to tell you their secrets. That's the acceptable direction for trust to travel. Just make sure you don't do any U-turns on that one-way street. Never ever trust your secrets to anyone with a tongue and a pulse. Be a reasonable skeptic or suffer the unreasonable escape of your secrets.

Trust is the femme fatale of human relationships. Trust will seduce you like Helen of Troy and create an epic catastrophe. Trust will draw you in like the Sirens and destroy your cover.

The Skeleton Key

There is some wisdom in the saying, "Beware of a door with too many keys." When that happens with your closet door, it might as well be a revolving door.

However, it's also vital that your closet locks are impervious to the workings of The Skeleton Key. This unique key has unlocked countless closet doors because it looks so harmless. It doesn't look like it would open anything, which is why it is so dangerous.

Remember, secrets, by their very nature, are more slippery than watermelon seeds at a hot July picnic. They hide quietly and then suddenly beg to be told, even when they are potential life changers. To protect your closet, you need to keep it safe from the hard-to-recognize *skeleton key* that will unlock your secrets and all the disaster they bring.

The Skeleton Key is difficult to identify as a threat because it masquerades as a virtue. It looks like the key to relational health. It looks like the key to mutual affection. You might even think it is the key to some significant happiness. It is, contrary to appearances, the key to catastrophe. It is the key to calamity.

You've heard of Tolkien's ring of power. Well, this is the key of doom. It is your enemy and your worst nightmare because it's a master key that opens every skeleton closet in existence. The key has a name. It's called Mutual Trust. It is the guard-dropping trust that develops when we are enveloped by a warm sense of being trusted by another.

Trust acts a bit like electricity. If it's only flowing in one direction, nothing happens. When the current moves in both directions, however, the light comes on, and you don't want that—closets and secrets are meant to stay in the darkness.

Let us be clear. We don't have an issue with trust as long as it's traveling one direction: from someone else to you. If you are a trustworthy person and your family member decides to bend your ear with something juicy, that's fine. You can put that secret in the bank in case you need it later. Family secrets make great levers.

Likewise, if your friend trusts you enough to spill their beans, consider it insurance as well as entertainment. Soak it up and share it with an out-of-town friend. The point is that appearing to be trustworthy so as to get a glimpse in someone else's closet is a fine way to make sure they don't try prying into yours. It's never a bad thing to hold onto someone else's skeleton key.

Just don't let them get yours! The key of doom is created when trust goes mutual, which it always tries to do. You must be on your guard even more when someone trusts you. There is a mesmerizing effect at work when this happens, as it leads you toward the infamous mutual trust massage and the exchange of keys. Don't fall for the pseudo-security of thinking your secret is safe with anyone just because they shared one with you. Whatever you do, don't trust Trust!

Yes, we know that trust can give you warm fuzzy feelings. That's the problem. Trust is as slippery as leather shoes on ice. One minute you're secrets are safely in your closet, and in a flash they have slipped out of control and you are on your backside in pieces. Mutual trust is the WD-40 of secrets. It goes to work loosening up even the tightest lips and closets.

Trust is a skeleton key you cannot afford to share. Your closet is too valuable and vulnerable for such carelessness. When someone shares a secret with you, it will come with an implicit invitation to do the same. Keep your own skeleton key hidden so well that even you can't get your hands on it!

Beware of friends who flatter you by trusting you with secrets. Remember the spider and the fly poem. These friends want you to "come into their parlor" of trust. But it's a Venus flytrap. They will suck the secrets right out of you. It seems like a relatively safe thing to do, but then the trap is sprung and it's too late. It's the undercover vice cop walking the street, waiting for some sucker to trust that she's only looking for fun and a little money. A good rule of thumb when you are being seduced by another's trust is to imagine that your "friend" works for the National Inquirer and records all your conversations.

Don't Underestimate Trust

You may think we are being alarmists, or hyperbolic like your parents tended to be when you were a kid. "Don't play with that or you'll poke your eye out!" We understand that you are skeptical about our call for skepticism, and we like that.

The truth is, however, that misplaced mutual trust has led to more exposure than all the bikinis in Rio. We aren't exaggerating when we advise you to treat trust like nitroglycerin.

In an earlier era, a baker came to suspect that he was being cheated. He didn't believe the farmer from whom he bought butter was giving him a pound of butter for a pound's price. So, he began to take the pound of butter home to weigh it and sure enough, he was getting short changed.

Irate that he had trusted the farmer, the baker sued for damages. When they appeared in court, the judge heard the baker's accusation and then turned to the farmer.

"Do you use standard weights when measuring out your goods," the judge asked?

"As a matter of fact, I don't," said the farmer, very calmly.

"Well then sir, would you mind explaining how you measure your goods?"

"Yes, your honor. When I measure out the baker's butter, I take a one pound loaf of bread that I buy from him and put it on the other side of my balance scale."

The moral of the story is more than "you cannot trust anyone." The moral is that mutual trust means secrets always come out in pairs: theirs and then yours. Half of that equation is unacceptable. You may resist the notion, but it is universally true. Unless you want people putting your secrets on their own morality scale, you best guard against any mutual trust. Keep the trust traffic moving in only one direction!

You must stay on your guard because trusting can sneak up on you. It can feel like being really comfortable with someone. You don't even realize your guard is dropping until it's down...which is too late. We will turn to some tips on keeping your guard up in a moment.

Here's the thing with you and your secrets: It can be a tough relationship, especially when the skeletons have been around for a long time and no longer give you any pleasure. Many of these secrets wear us down, harass us, and otherwise hang things over our heads. This makes us vulnerable and anxious.

Whenever we are anxious about a relationship or situation, like the one hiding in our closet, there is a powerful tendency to offload that anxiety onto someone else. Anxiety builds like steam in a teapot. Eventually, that teapot needs to release the pressure, and that's when it starts to sing.

Psychologists call this release triangulation. *When our secrets cause too much pressure and there is a release valve like a "trusted" friend, we start to sing like that teapot.* The feeling is that we are easing the pressure, but this is a delusion. Triangulation doesn't diminish our anxiety at all. It multiplies it by releasing it into an echo chamber of exposure.

When someone else trusts you, you begin to think it might feel good to let him or her know what you've been dragging around and locking up. But trust us. As soon as that toothpaste is out of the tube, you'll never get it back in. You will regret it as soon as the words are out of your mouth, and your secret is suddenly out of your control.

Don't give in. That friend who seems trustworthy when you are in a weak moment would love nothing better than to podcast your delicious secret at the earliest opportunity. As soon as you begin to share, they will begin to pull more and more out of your closet. Once you open Pandora's box, you cannot keep anything inside.

It's a tragic reality. What initially feels like relief from your burden will suddenly feel like a new disaster from which you need relief! You think your sister was a master at blackmail…you haven't seen anything until a "frenemy" has the goods on you. Don't worry, they'll only tell a few others who promise to keep the secret.

The Vulnerability Vaccine

In order to help you build immunity against trusting others, especially when they trust you, we have developed a vulnerability vaccine. It is designed to protect you from being or acting vulnerable in any way. While not approved by the FDA, these suggestions are safe and effective. Trust us.

Our vaccination practices, found only here in *The Skeleton Code*, work in much the same way as their common flu or measles counterparts.

These relational skills and practices will give you just enough of the weakness called Vulnerability that your mind will develop a resistance to the full-blown version.

Using our vaccine principles may cause some minor or local irritation, but this will pass. We must also warn you that no vaccine is 100% effective, so even if you use our immunotherapy, you could put yourself in a bad position, have a sudden onset of trust, and spill your beans and secrets.

For the best protection, we suggest reading and contemplating the following list and placing it somewhere you are likely to see throughout the day. It's also helpful to revisit the immunity principles before any one-on-one meetings, especially with people you could be tempted to trust or with whom you might feel vulnerable.

We will use a format where the common (and unhelpful) principle of trust is given, followed by our vaccinated version designed to keep you in a position of strength and control. Common trust principles are intended to foster mutual trust in relationships and often promote personal vulnerability, so they are dangerous. Read these first statements for warning only and then focus on our ingenious alternative principles for immunity.

Remember, the Immunity Principle is the weakened version that will protect you from being vulnerable to full-blown trust.

Common Principle: Focus on the situation, issue, or behavior, not on the person.

Immunity Principle: Focus on other people's situations, issues, or behaviors, never your own.

At work, Brenda acts like a good and empathetic listener who would never judge. She seems only interested in work matters, but this invites the trust of others, even as she withholds her own.

Tip: Prepare some deflective comments around the theme, "It's not about me." Regardless of the situation, it's always altruistic to be concerned about the other person. When someone trusts you and shares something personal, they will often want to hear the same from you. Be ready with phrases that rest on the premise that "you" are not the real matter of importance. This is an expression of humility. Turn the conversation back to concern about the "other."

Common Principle: Maintain constructive relationships.

Immunity Principle: Maintain unilateral and controlled relationships where trust flows only from others to you.

It doesn't hurt to have relationships that work for you in your personal life, but be careful at work. Leaders are trying to leverage relationships in order to get more productivity from their workers, making them vulnerable to collegiality and trust.

Tip: Develop a list of quasi-personal stories or traits that promote your persona and protect your secrets. Use these strategically and others will assume you are being transparent. Stories of minor failures make you appear human and accessible: a failed marriage or business idea, for instance. Never deviate from your prepared list, however.

Common Principle: Take initiative to make things better.

Immunity Principle: Make things better to protect your privacy.

Improved relationships should serve to make your secrets more secure. It's fine to take initiative to help the friend, employer, or colleague. It's fine to take risks and admit mistakes at work to gain credibility, or in friendships to get brownie points.

Tip: Take on additional projects at home or at work to create a buffer for your privacy. If there's one thing Americans respect, it's being busy. When you are busy doing something important, others are less likely to engage you in small talk and otherwise pry into your life.

Common Principle: Lead by example.

Immunity Principle: Lead without vulnerability.

In a work environment, you can be a great example as long as your modeling doesn't include actual personal openness. Creating the illusion of openness can be helpful if it helps others trust you. Make sure that trust is one-way.

Tip: Read a book or attend a conference on leadership. These are rich repositories for stories that can work for you. You'll find some that seem to fit your own story. File them in your mind and have them ready to use when others might share personal examples. The emotional distance of using someone else's story is the key to success.

Common Principle: Think beyond the moment.

Immunity Principle: Protect your version of the future.

Exposure ruins futures—you must carry this in the front of your mind every day. Inspired by your Skeleton Code goals, you can be an inspiration to others to think about their future and their goals. Helping others focus on the future has the added benefit of redirecting them from your past.

Tip: Beware of people in therapy. They like introspection about their past and it's an easy jump to your past. Keep the focus on what the other person has experienced and learned. Remember their major issues and challenges. Use the phrase, "tell me more about..." and they will gladly talk about themselves.

What One-Way Trust Looks Like

Hopefully, you will take a good dose of the Trust Vaccine and develop the necessary immunity to keep you safe from trusting others with your secrets. If you are the trusting type, you may think this standard is beyond your reach. Take heart. Many have learned to be trusted without trusting in return.

Missy's obsession with young singers began when she was a preteen. She always had posters of her heartthrobs hanging in her bedroom. She literally covered the walls with Hanson, The Backstreet Boys, The Jonas Brothers, and New Kids on the Block.

When other teens her age were growing out of that phase and getting interested in local boys, Missy seemed to be going deeper into her fantasies. Instead of idolizing older singers, her attention was always focused on the youngest stars. In addition to poster-lined walls, she moved into the electronic era of obsession, spending hours on the websites of her unrequited lovers.

While she was in college, and living with roommates, she had to tone down the public displays, and so her connections became exclusively electronic, as evidenced by her home screen, photos, and bookmarks. She knew she had some form of celebrity worship syndrome, but didn't think it was pathological.

When she left college and moved into her own apartment, she became more fixated on her infatuations. But instead of the previous serial crushes on boy bands, she became absorbed with one artist. Every other poster came down. All the other links and photos were deleted. It did not matter that she was older than Justin Bieber, because he looked right into her soul. And she could see inside his, beneath all the boyish looks and bad boy behavior. She had a copy of every picture of Justin that had ever been published.

If someone had seen Missy's bedroom at the time, they would have had two reactions. First, they would think of those who practice ancestor worship, as the room was nothing short of a shrine to Justin. The second thought would probably have been, *I better call the police*, because the whole scene had "stalker" written all over it.

Yet Missy was not a stalker. She was not dangerous, just deluded. Her bedroom was, however, a grade-A secret that she could not share with anyone, including her favorite niece, Julia, who happened to be a big Justin Bieber fan.

The crucial moment came when Missy took her niece to a Bieber concert. When they came back to Missy's apartment, Julia was all over Missy's collection of Justin Bieber books adorning the coffee table. She even told her aunt Missy that she was in love with Justin.

Thankfully, Missy understood the danger of getting lulled into a mutual admiration society. She kept her skeleton key secure and her trust to herself, resisting the idea that she could share her bedroom shrine with Julia.

There are no innocent practices of trust. There are no secure ways to exchange skeleton keys. Once you give that key to someone else, you'll never get it back. And even if you do, they will have made a copy at Home Depot.

We agree with Walter Cronkite who always said, "And that's the way it is." He was right. That's the way it is with people. They will tell you how much they love you. They will say, "Don't worry, you can trust me." They might even share their secret with you. Beware. When someone trusts you, you need a powerful dose of immunity.

In Summary

All the bleeding hearts of the world want us to trust each other. They think the world would be a better place if we all practiced vulnerability. Trusting someone with your secrets is like trusting ISIS with your homeland security. It's insanity.

Trust worshipers want you to be vulnerable so that you will trust them and they will be in the position of power. Don't join this human relations bandwagon if you have any serious skeletons. Instead, practice these immunity principles:

1. **Keep Trust Moving In Only One Direction In Relationships**: Toward You. Be as trustworthy as you can, but don't let it become mutual.

2. **Operate From A Relational Base of Skepticism: Always.** Don't just be dubious about your friend or co-worker; be skeptical about your own tendencies to trust.

3. **Important Relationships Require Greater Immunity.** If your façade is going to crack, it will probably happen with someone who is close, so keep your armor on.

4. **Keep A Very Close Eye On Your Skeleton Key.** There are many ways secrets can slip out of our closets in a heartbeat, especially when we feel an unrealistic sense of security. Keep a good grip on your closet key when you are around people you like.

5. **Find Non-Human Avenues To Vent.** Everyone feels pressure from their secrets and at times will think they should let off some steam with a trusted friend. Don't give in to this impulse. Instead, vent by banging weights at the gym, hitting a punching bag, shooting animals, yelling at referees, buying too many shoes, hammering a nail, or some similar activity that keeps your expression on a sub-human level.

6. **Stay Immune From Vulnerability**, which is a Venus flytrap. Being vulnerable is the proverbial straight line: the shortest distance between security and exposure.

We know that our Skeleton Code strategies will be a stretch for you. Keeping secrets safe is hard work and there are no shortcuts. We also know that all work and no play can leave us vulnerable to silly mistakes and sloppy security. That's why we propose delightful distractions in our next chapter. Read on.

Chapter Seven

Personal Distraction

*It's important to figure out how much toxicity you can
tolerate while still being able to live the life you want.*
—Coach Chinh

In the preceding chapters, we have challenged you to implement several
Skeleton Code strategies that will greatly improve your closet security.
Keeping secrets safe is vital to your personal success. However, just
like rest is integral to the training regimen of an athlete, so is personal
downtime from the responsibilities of closet maintenance an essential
component of your overall success.

Even if you have only begun to implement a few of the secret-
securing techniques we've set forth thus far, you are likely feeling the
weight of the long-term effort required to maintain your closet. We do

not see the value in candy-coating the challenges of successful secret keeping. Let's be realistic about the stress of constantly watching over a well-kept closet. This chapter is not about diverting others from your skeletons, but finding some helpful distractions from the constant strain of skeleton maintenance. In reality, fresh lips don't sink as many ships!

A mother of five children, aged seven and younger, was flying overseas to join her military husband who had been reassigned to a base in Germany. Having flown through the very long night with all her children and baggage, the mother was moving her little chickadees toward the cramped customs area. A young customs officer watched in disbelief as they approached in a cloud of dust.

"Good morning Ma'am," he said. "Do all these children and does all this luggage belong to you?"

"Yes sir," she said. "They're all mine."

He smiled and then began his well-rehearsed set of questions.

"Ma'am, do you have any weapons, contraband, or illegal drugs in your possession?

The mother blew a strand of hair from her face, shifted her crying 9-month-old to her other hip and said, "Son, if I had any of those things, don't you think I would have used them by now?"

The customs officer sent her on her way.

Most of us have seen how worn-out mothers crack under pressure. It's not a pretty sight. But not even the worst three-year-old can wipe you out like an exposed secret! That's why a closet respite is required.

When we are chronically or overly stressed, not only is our function and intellect compromised, we are also two to three times as likely to let our secrets slip. When we have a closet with even one significant skeleton, we need to achieve a reasonable level of balance in our lives so we can maintain the strategies and techniques that keep our secrets safe.

Some of our serious skeletons can drain us like a houseful of preschoolers. As we discuss elsewhere in this book, they like to rattle around and escape from time to time. Managing them according to the Code can consume a great deal of your time and energy. You need to maintain some equilibrium.

We make many more mistakes when we don't have mental and emotional safety valves. You cannot guard your secrets 24/7/365. You need some personal escape, some emotional space, and some well-planned diversions.

Protected Diversions

As you are diverting others from your secrets in order to live the life you want, you will also need to divert your own attention from that unfortunate lapse or ongoing duplicity that caused your closet crisis in the first place. And if you've done a good job of minding your closet, why shouldn't you treat yourself to a personal diversion?

But you can't just walk away from your closet anymore than you can walk away from your job when you go on vacation. To get out of town the right way, you need to leave an "out of office" reply. You need to reschedule the meeting. You need to think ahead before you leave so your co-worker doesn't have to dig through your files in order to find the invoice you were supposed to send out. It takes the same forethought to walk away from your closet for any period of time.

Dr. Wes wasn't making the good money a doctor should because many of his patients were on Medicaid, and those payments are much lower than those provided by private insurance. But he had learned to make lemonade from the lemons. He simply billed Medicaid for some extra services he did not actually deliver. It was a lucrative process that beat taking an extra shift at the hospital.

It was also a secret that required fulltime attention, especially when the good doctor's office was open and other staff members were utilizing files and computers. Even when the doctor was not creating phony files, he was using a good deal of energy to guard his skeletons.

Dr. Wes knew how to divert others away from his secrets, but he also recognized the need to develop a personal diversion strategy. He had to close his office and get out of town in order to get a break from managing his interesting life. Only in some remote location could he relax and spend the fruit of his secret life.

Notice that we said he closed his office. He could not risk some employee sifting through his files while he was gone. You need a diversion from skeleton maintenance, but it must not expose you to unnecessary risk, or it fails in its purpose.

Often, our secrets are problematic and even more exhausting because we do not have a strategy for keeping them safe when we are "out of town." Using The Skeleton Code to develop an effective plan will allow you take an occasional break from this important work.

The break is important to recharge your batteries, but you simply cannot walk away from your closet without a care. You wouldn't dream of going on vacation without locking your house and turning on your alarm system. You can always board your dog when you go away, but there are no such accommodations for skeletons like those "medicinal" plants you have growing behind your garage.

Yes, pursue personal diversions, but not until you have taken the appropriate precautions with your skeleton closet. If you have done that, and if you need a break from your more nefarious secrets, here are four premium Skeleton Code guidelines to make sure you have some great and safe diversions. Practice these and you'll escape the pressures of secret keeping for a while. Then you'll come home rejuvenated and ready to keep protecting that persona of yours.

Two Green Lights For Personal Diversion

1. Find Some Socially Acceptable Pleasures.

Because you can always add more skeletons to your collection if you are bored, we recommend finding some outlets that require no maintenance.

We know, this sounds like acquiescence, but hear us out. We don't want you over-indulged so that your closet gets too full and unmanageable. It's like having too many kids.

You need some balance in your life, and this can be provided when you spend a little time engaging in thoughts and actions that meet basic social standards in your context. We all need to participate in some communal form of customary and conventional activities.

Many of these activities are published in local newspapers or magazines. You might also get new ideas from some of your fun-loving co-workers, though you probably want to avoid places frequented by acquaintances.

The point is to take a break from the activities and inclinations that created your skeletons in the first pace. You don't always have to be tempting other women's husbands or experimenting with new vices. You could take up horseback riding, for instance, and enjoy physical contact with an animal that's more socially acceptable.

The added benefit of choosing more modest activities is that others see you in these settings. This gives you character points, or at least "normalcy" points.

We know it sounds strange, but some people actually find pleasure in conventional hobbies, though there are many boring options to sort through. Yes, it requires some effort, but finding the right choices can really reduce your stress. Find something that fits your conventional personality.

You don't have to push the envelope. One does not need to engage in base jumping or hang-gliding, for instance, to get the benefits of diversion, though some personality types need this adrenaline just to stay awake.

James, a 22-year-old would-be stunt man, tried to add to his resume by bungee jumping off the Clifton Suspension Bridge in Bristol, England. His own diversion from the standard jump was to light himself on fire. His plan was to use a knife to cut the cord so he would then plunge into the river below to extinguish the flames.

Everything worked at first, though he discovered while bobbing up and down that his knife was not sharp enough to cut the cord quickly. Instead of a few seconds, he dangled burning for almost half a minute before falling into the river.

A spokesperson for the Dangerous Sports Club told the BBC, "His heart is in the right place, but stunt men usually put on flame-retardant suits."

James was able to spend some diversionary time in a nice burn unit where he did recover, though he should probably try to keep that whole episode in his closet.

We think secret keeping is a type of risky behavior, so why not take a break from the edgy stuff when you try to take a break from your closet? There are other options that don't require so much effort.

Sports are sacrosanct in our culture. There are limitless opportunities to participate in or observe athletics. These activities are designed to help you project your own fears, dreams, and frustrations onto athletes and referees, so they make great escapes from the skeletons that demand your attention or drag you down.

The same can be said for shopping. We have clients who spend many satisfying hours imagining what they would own if they didn't have to pay their VISA bill. This activity does have some risk, however, if you have one of many store fetishes.

Jessica really needed a diversion and thought she'd try her hand at bowling. She had a friend who was deep into the sport and was always nagging her about it. She decided giving it a try would get the friend off her back and give her a little exercise in the process.

Unfortunately, bowling, unlike more private sports such as golf, is done in a very large room full of people. This was problematic for two reasons. First, Jessica's secret was her previous occupation as an undercover cop working in vice, which was quite a contrast to her current and more private vocation of being an executive chef.

Apparently, many of the men who frequented certain parts of town in the evenings looking for companionship, also frequented bowling alleys on other nights of the week. As it turned out, the guy who ran the league had been arrested for propositioning her. Recognizing these former "acquaintances" didn't help her relax and move on, so she had to try something else.

It usually does take some trial and error before you find an acceptable pleasure that fits your own needs. It's ok to try something once and then set it aside to find something else. We do suggest looking outside those old areas of interest that created your secrets in the first place.

While it is socially acceptable, and even preferable for many, we discourage our clients from spending extended time on social media when they are trying to get some rest. As we have said, electronic information is not anonymous and it never goes away. It can also become addictive, putting your secrets at greater risk over time. Engaging in social media also requires you to be on high alert, which defeats the purpose of relaxing disengagement.

Remember, if you live in a big city, check out the "Living" section of your local paper or a newcomer magazine for activity and event ideas. If you live in a smaller town, it might be better to shop for some diversions offered in neighboring cities so you can avoid getting caught up in the amusement of small-town gossip.

2. Find Entertainment With People You'll Never See Again.

While close friends can be nice, they also require work. It's that whole close but not-too-close tension that is sometimes more trouble than it's worth. As we shared in the last chapter, trust can be a security liability with friends.

Strangers, on the other hand, are refreshingly anonymous and can be much more useful when it comes to a personal diversion. Many have discovered this advantage by going on a cruise: alone of course. In such a setting, you can be yourself, knowing you won't ever have to see those people again. It's a really delightful freedom.

Rick has old racist thoughts that still bubble up from his upbringing in the Deep South. While he has a great job in liberal and multicultural Boston, his racial bias gets triggered on a regular basis. Sometimes, he can't keep the thoughts inside and they come out as mutterings.

This emotional tic is a real problem for two reasons. First, Rick doesn't want to be a racist. He doesn't tell racist jokes and doesn't mistreat people of color that he actually meets. His feelings and impulses are involuntary reactions that involve distant encounters with strangers.

Rick wonders if these people actually know him and follow him around town, it happens so often. A car with windows down rolls up beside him at a traffic light. He feels the shockwaves of that car's turbo bass rattling his windows and drowning out his jazz. He hears lyrics that violate his southern sensibilities, and the slurs and epithets flood into his head with as much force as the unwelcomed beat. While this annoys him no matter the race of the other driver, he knows the feelings are more intense if the driver is African-American.

Rick can't risk talking to anyone about this. He works in an office alongside several African-Americans, none of whom trigger his racist feelings. In fact, whatever progress he has made moving beyond his old biases is due to the people of color he has known in his adult life. Even so, Rick lives in chronic fear that in some other setting, like an office lunch or retreat, something might slip out and be overheard by one of his colleagues.

Rick needs a diversion from his secret and has found New Hampshire to be a great getaway spot. He doesn't know anyone there and in the three times he's visited, he hasn't seen a person of color yet!

There are so many advantages to getaways that put you with people you'll never see again. You don't even have to use a false identity, as long as you don't give out any personal information. In these settings, you can be who you want to be for a few days and then leave all the relationships and cares behind.

Adventure trips are another option if you like that pace, as are vacations to other countries. What happens in Italy stays in Italy! We don't know about Vegas.

Let us offer you some quick anonymous getaway ideas:

- Many cruises are brief and affordable, not to mention anonymous.
- Many sports clubs allow guests to participate in rides or events at least once. Check your local listings.
- Cooking classes are offered in many fine cities and resort locations, and can last from 3 hours to 3 days. You can actually tell people about these adventures.
- Festivals, festivals, festivals. They are everywhere and are always happening, but be careful if you have a drug weakness.
- Continuing Education. Many of these opportunities can be great fun, and you can develop a new expertise in the process, or at least some diversionary conversation points.

Two Red Lights For Personal Diversion

1. Don't Attend Support Groups.

We cannot overstress this warning. Secrets and support groups are like sodium and water—a really volatile combination. Any group that strives for honesty in a nonjudgmental context is a danger zone for people who have secrets to keep.

It doesn't matter the purpose of the group or how many steps they have, these groups lull you into a false sense of trust. People in support groups make you believe that you would be accepted even if your secrets were known. It's a trap! People who reveal their shadow selves think everyone else should do the same, and they won't rest until they convince you to crack that closet door.

Bobbie's daughter was diagnosed with autism. Parenting is difficult enough without the added dimension of a significant difference or disability. Not only was she a single mother, Bobbie also lived far away from family members who might have helped.

A doctor treating her daughter suggested a support group. It was composed of other mothers dealing with the challenges of parenting a child with autism. Bobbie was tired, stressed, and frustrated, so she grasped the straw.

Any group that strives for honesty in a nonjudgmental context is a danger zone for people who have secrets to keep.

Everything seemed to be going fine for the first few months. Bobbie liked the facilitator and the other participants in the group. They seemed genuine and she felt supported and encouraged. Others shared very personal struggles and after a time, Bobbie felt that she could do the same.

Sharing was the key, they said. But she didn't realize that the key to her feelings about parenting her child was also the key that would unlock a different closet—one she needed to keep closed.

You see, Bobbie had played a major role in the CIA's MKULTRA Program, where detainees were subjected to enhanced interrogation or torture, depending on your definition. She had been a Med-Tec at one of the secret facilities, administering LSD and other mind-altering drugs, as well as trying to keep the detainees alive in the course of their drawn out interrogations.

Not only did she not object to the methods used, she tried to err on the side of reckless abandon when it came to "those creatures" as she called them. On at least two occasions, she had ok'd the continuation of waterboarding that culminated in the death of a detainee. At least three others suffered brain damage from the asphyxia.

Bobbie had lost a brother on 9/11. He was a firefighter and first responder. Even though she didn't feel conflicted about her methods at the time, after coming home those feelings changed and she certainly didn't want her family to know of her involvement.

She knew she could not share her past with anyone, but it came out anyway. While she was in a vulnerable state, sharing with her group, she spilled the beans. So now there are 14 new people in her town who have seen what's in her closet. Who knows where it will go from there?

If it can happen to a disciplined operative, it can happen to you. Avoid support groups! Instead of diversion, you'll get disaster.

2. Avoid Introspection.

As we have said, you deserve a respite from guarding your skeletons 24/7, but this does not mean you can shift into neutral. There's an old saying about idle hands being the "devil's workshop." Idle minds are the same. Personal diversion is about keeping your mind busy with a different set of interests or challenges, not letting your mind engage in any type of personal reflection. Always maintain an outward mental focus, especially when you're taking a skeleton vacation.

You need to stay busy and distracted or your secrets will keep interrupting your joyful getaway. And remember, letting your mind move toward any form of self-evaluation is a perfect prescription for guilt trips, shame trips, doubt trips, and depression trips. Wouldn't a trip to San Francisco be so much better?

Because self-examination is not your friend, we must discourage you from certain practices like yoga and reading self-help books (except this one, of course). If you must do yoga for the physical benefits, listen to 50 Cent instead of harp music because his music lives on the opposite side of the planet from meditation. You might also watch Dr. Phil while you're putting yourself into the shape of a pretzel. You know those people on his show are *really* screwed up, and that's entertainment.

If you must curl up with a book, make it a murder mystery or romance novel (or this book). If you must pray, do so for the benefit of your children when sitting down to a nice meal. The smell of good food will always keep those prayers brief and superficial. Prayers before exams (school and medical) are also pretty safe. If you must take a quiet walk, make sure you're keeping your mind busy with something external like an audio book (perhaps this one).

Some people ask whether it's safe to attend church or synagogue. In most cases and places, this is not a problem. Religious communities are some of the most fractured places on Earth, and they're usually hiding more secrets than you are. Plus, most everyone is just going through the motions. Larger faith communities are preferable because you can remain detached or even anonymous while giving the appearance of being upstanding. Just stay away from any small groups that major on relationships or spiritual vulnerability. Doing social benevolence is okay because this compliments the persona you need to fulfill other Skeleton Code strategies.

Beware of navel gazing, reflection, meditation, contemplation, or any other activities that open your heart or mind to self-evaluation and therefore make you more defenseless.

Maryann had a difficult childhood. Her parents divorced when she was young and they continued to fight from their separate houses—a very uncivil war. Everyone but Maryann understood why she struggled in school. She quickly learned that she needed some way to compensate for her poor grades, and the method she learned and perfected was cheating.

It started off as an occasional glance during a test, only when she knew the answer but wasn't completely sure. Of course, it became a pattern as she grew less sure of herself and as the material became more difficult. She was able to get into college, but had to develop better techniques to get by. These included cheat sheets and elaborate schemes to take tests in the offices of professors, where she was often left unattended.

It always surprised Maryann that she didn't seem inclined to cheat on taxes, in her marriage, or at work. It was just school, and it made her feel terribly guilty. She needed a diversion from her secret, but instead chose to engage it head on.

With too much stress and time to navel gaze about her guilt, she made an impulsive decision. She contacted her college, confessed her misdeeds in a letter, and told officials she was shredding her diploma. She received a rather abrupt letter in reply from the Office of Academic Affairs noting that the appropriate changes would be made to university records and transcripts. Maryann felt some relief, but it was short-lived.

A month later, she lost her job. As she set out to create a new resume, she suddenly realized that it would contain a gaping hole, and she was seized by fear. No one would hire her for the work she did without a college degree, and her transcript was now only a figment of her imagination.

Too bad that Maryann was lulled into a false security because of her careless navel-gazing and impulsive act of conscience. Her guilt was an annoyance, but nothing like the disaster of her open secret. She should have had a glass of wine for her guilt instead. If so, she would probably have a decent job and not the retail position she took instead. Now she's stuck in her self-made Purgatory, and it all started with needing a break and too much careless navel-gazing.

You need a break from your skeletons to be sure, but you don't need to understand or psychoanalyze them by letting them lay down on your couch. Lock them up and do something fun instead. Just make sure it's not too fun or you'll have another skeleton to guard.

A Strategy, Not A Luxury

Engaging in personal distractions is a vital secret keeping strategy just like mimicking the political masters or dressing for diversion. Don't think of it as a luxury you can afford to live without.

In his book, *They Call Me Coach*, John Wooden says, "it's always been my philosophy to follow our game plan no matter what the score happens to be. I caution our teams, play your game—just play your game. This does not mean we will always outscore our opponents. But it does ensure that we will *not beat ourselves*" (added emphasis).

We know too many people who have lost more than a game because they beat themselves as secret-keepers. They got stuck in their own closets and didn't know how to take a break. They needed some time on the bench, but tried to stay in the game all the time. It won't work.

Come up with a quality game plan for some diversions and stick to it. The money you spend will be well worth it. You can keep your secrets safe if you don't beat yourself. Remember, we don't make good decisions when we're under too much pressure. Instead, we buy timeshares and boats and regret it for years.

Listen to Coach Wooden. If you don't beat yourself, you'll be able to stay ahead of the game for a long time to come.

Your good energy and emotional balance will be essential as we move into the next *Skeleton Code* chapter, because if you are too drained or stressed, you'll not be able to manage the challenge. With toxic closets, your alternatives are evolution or extinction.

So get rejuvenated and get ready to get better: to move into the highest levels of secret keeping. As with many other disciplines, you are either progressing or regressing. If your closet "technology" is not doubling in quality each year, it's failing. So take a deep breath, put the pedal down, and accelerate into the fast lane of personal prowess.

Chapter Eight

Get Better Or Get Caught

Continuous effort, not strength or intelligence,
is the key to unlocking our potential.
—Winston Churchill

At this point, we have covered seven keys to skeleton security and we hope that you are putting these strategies into practice. What we want to communicate in this chapter is that real security requires consistent improvement in all of the areas we have identified. Skeleton maintenance is like technology—if it isn't evolving, it's becoming a liability. If you aren't getting better at keeping your secrets secure, you are becoming more vulnerable by the day.

Don't underestimate the Houdini nature of your secrets. They can squeeze and squirm their way out of the most robust slammer. Secrets can act like a damsel in distress, locked away in the dungeon, needing to be rescued. Remember your role here. You're not the white knight. You're the Lord Chancellor and Keeper of the Keys. Yes, those secrets will call out to you promising understanding and forgiveness if only you will set them free. Don't be fooled by their temptations and machinations.

Little Sally was wearing a frilly, lacy dress on Easter and was obviously very happy with her look. The minister noticed her that morning and said, "Sally, that is a lovely dress you're wearing. Did your mom buy that for you?" To which Sally replied, "No, this is the dress my mommy had when she was a little girl."

"Well isn't that wonderful," said the minister.

"I don't think so," said Sally. "I heard her say it was a bitch to iron."

That's the deal with skeletons, too. You can't make them presentable, no matter how much you try to iron them out. So get better at keeping them safe, or get caught in the emotional crossfire of your life.

Wake Up and Smell The Closet

Success in secret keeping requires not only dedication and improvement, but also good insight into the changing landscape of personal information and security. Keeping a secret in the age of social media requires much greater attention and vision than was needed by previous generations.

In this chapter, we will challenge you to get better at all the principles of privacy we have identified so you don't fall into exposure. This will require some new self-awareness about what makes you lackadaisical in your closet security. We will also help move you beyond satisfaction with your current practices that are growing stale, coaching you to conceptualize new skills that make the most of cutting edge brain science. Tape this quote from Napoleon Hill to your mirror: *Strength and growth come only through continuous effort and struggle.*

Many of us are infected with the illusion that destiny is on our side. You may be satisfied that your buried secret is secure because someone or something, like the Easter Bunny or Tooth Fairy, is looking out for you. Maybe you had childhood experiences of a mother or grandfather covering for you when you messed things up. Get this out of your head. No one is going to bail you out.

A seven-year-old boy named Tim was sitting at his school desk needing to go to the bathroom, but trying to wait until recess. The teacher was in the middle of a lesson and he didn't want to interrupt, but he couldn't wait and disaster struck. Beyond his control, a puddle formed on the floor beneath him.

Tim was in a state of panic. When the other boys found out what he did, he would be the laughing stock. When the girls found out, they would never speak to him again.

Tim put his head down on his desk and asked God to take him home to heaven. His life was over. When he looked up, the teacher was walking toward him and he knew the end had come.

Suddenly, however, a classmate named Suzie was moving down the aisle beside him with a plastic goldfish bowl. She stumbled and all the water in that bowl landed right in Tim's lap. He pretended to be angry but inside, he was saying, "Thank you God."

Now, instead of being the object of ridicule, Tim was the object of sympathy. He was dismissed to go change into some gym shorts while the school called his mother for some dry clothes. As life would have it, the ridicule that should have been his was transferred to Suzie. She tried to help clean up but everyone told her just to stay out of the way. They called her a klutz.

At the end of the day, as children waited for their buses, Tim approached Suzie and whispered to her, "You did that on purpose didn't you?" Suzie whispered back, "I wet my pants once too."

Wake up and smell the closet! This is sweet, syrupy fiction! It's total fantasy and it isn't ever going to happen to you. Children don't act this way when they see peers screw up, and it gets even less likely as we age.

None of your adult friends will show up to protect you from exposure. No one is going to shield you from the takedown. You'll be busted, humiliated, and ruined if you ever drop your guard or leave that closet door ajar.

The first step toward getting better and not getting caught is to confront this fairytale notion that everything will be fine even if you just keep doing what you're doing. If your friend harasses you to quit smoking, you'll probably just get irritated, but if your physician tells you to quit or you'll have a heart attack, you'll probably shift into gear. That's the gear we want you to find so you'll get better at keeping your secrets safe.

> Your closet may have been an imposing skeleton safe at one time, but if it's not keeping up with the times, it's moving toward dinosaur status just like your reputation.

Trust us: closet complacency is dangerous and widespread. The longer our skeletons remain locked away, the more we become lulled into that infamous false sense of security. The easier the secret was hidden in the first place, the easier we think it will be to keep it there.

Evolution or Extinction

Dinosaurs were some of the most impressive animals ever to populate our planet. Notice the past tense. We now use the term "dinosaur" as a euphemism to describe, "that which is outdated and useless."

Your closet may have been an imposing skeleton safe at one time, but if it's not keeping up with the times, it's moving toward dinosaur status just like your reputation.

Once John got the IT job and salary he wanted and had settled into his life trajectory, he forgot that he had inserted a little extra experience into his resume. It was such a simple deception.

Years before, John had become more desperate in his job search after getting nowhere in the market for weeks. He knew he would interview well, but was hitting a wall with HR departments before he ever made it to that all-important job phase. It was so frustrating.

His resume just didn't stand out and he knew it. He had great work experience, but not for a notable company. He had seen an article about the importance of resume "bells and whistles," but on paper his experience didn't ring or sing.

Eventually, he gave in and made some changes. John decided to replace his three-year stint in a start-up (that didn't make it) with some noteworthy experience at Google. He had a friend who worked there who could serve as a "reference" if anyone called. In the end, it's always who you know!

So John's resume finally stood out and soon he got the interview he had been waiting for… followed by that really good job. He kicked himself for not making the move sooner. No one had bothered to dig into his work background; only the usual criminal and drug check.

An interesting thing happened in John's mind as he settled into his job. After all the prep he had done to convince others of his exceptional work experience, it was as if he had actually been there and done that with Google. He had only changed the location on his resume, not the work and expertise itself. It no longer seemed like a padded Vitae at all. Plus, he figured that his secret was safely locked away in some HR file cabinet.

Had John put forth the same creative effort in protecting his secret as he did in creating it, all would have been well. He should have evolved. Twice a year, his supervisor held his personnel file during evaluations. John could have easily pulled his embellished resume and replaced it with a factual one.

But he didn't do that because he thought it was "all good." John never imagined that, five years down the road, his company would hire someone as his supervisor who had actually worked at Google during the same time period that appeared on his resume. This someone also liked to know everything about the people who worked for her, so she looked at their files. Had John been prepared for this possibility (see chapter on Plausible Deniability), he might have avoided the eventual disaster that followed.

The status quo will not keep your skeletons at bay. You must be proactive to keep secrets. Holding the line will leave you holding a bag of bones. If you coast, you're toast! Sleeping dogs don't lie down forever. Skeletons get restless. They like to come out and play. Old strategies for keeping secrets just don't last. Those are all the clichés we can think of…

Keep improving your security, or expect a new Ice Age for your once proud image.

A Game Of Inches

They say that golf is a game of inches, but we don't know any sports that aren't decided by the narrowest of margins. Two inches can separate a first down from a turnover on downs. Three inches can separate a foul ball from a home run, and five inches is the difference between a gold medal Biathlon marksman and an amateur. The game of secrecy is no different. It just takes one little miss to make a mess.

When Ken was a kid, his cousin Tom bought a switchblade knife on a family trip to Mexico. It was hidden in his room because he bought it without his parents' knowledge. Ken didn't believe his secret until Tom opened a box from the back of a drawer and held up that black and silver marvel. When Tom pushed the button, the blade swung out faster than lightning. Ken's mouth was wide open in awe.

Ken reached for it and Tom said, "Be careful… it will cut your finger off," which only made Ken want it more.

Later, Ken asked his mom, the softer of his parents, if he could get a switchblade knife. It seemed like a reasonable request at the time (age 9).

"I promise I'll be real careful with it and won't ever take it to school." (Right)

"I'm afraid that's out of the question," his mother said with a smile. "Young boys don't have any business with switchblade knives."

"Yes we do," Ken protested. "You can ask Tom!"

"And how would your cousin know this?"

"Well…I don't know…but maybe Tom has read about it…I mean… can you forget I said that? (*Note: Tom still thinks his sister ratted on him.*)

Secrets can slip out of your own mouth just like that, even when you haven't had too much to drink. It doesn't just happen to excitable kids. It happens to sober adults, perky adults, stressed out adults, worn out adults, and bored adults.

Yes, we are beating this drum over and over because everyone gets in a rut with secrets. Remember, it was not a lack of intelligence that led to the security breach and attack on September 11th. According to The 9/11 Commission, it was a lack of imagination. We had the raw intelligence data but just could not put it together. Government agencies and systems did not communicate effectively enough to discern and thwart the threat.

Skeleton security does not require exceptional intelligence, but it does require great imagination and superior coordination of all closet strategies. Otherwise, you miss the threat to your image by inches, which more often than not is a real game-changer.

Doing What It Takes

Each of the strategies for skeleton security we address in this book will require a commitment to self-improvement. We hope you are not overwhelmed by how much you need to learn and grow in these pursuits, and we are happy to share that many others have risen from the ranks of mediocrity to excellence. You can do this too.

Consider, for instance, the creative genius of Pablo Picasso, who has influenced artists and non-artists alike. Picasso illustrated the spirit of personal improvement when he said; *I am always doing that which I cannot do, in order that I may learn how to do it.*

Don't worry if you're a novice. Don't give up if you've never kept your secrets like a pro. You can learn. You can get better. You can secure that closet for years to come.

It is reported that in his later years, Picasso would enter an art gallery where his work was on display. After looking over a piece that caught his eye, he would pull out his paint and brush and begin to make changes to his own art. Eventually, curators would not allow him to roam the gallery unattended. For some reason, they didn't appreciate his commitment to excellence and constant improvement.

Yet this is the kind of surreal devotion skeleton security requires. The work of keeping secrets, like keeping a well-manicured lawn, is never done. Good closet security doesn't work if it's on again off again. There are always new ways to strengthen your locks and secure your future.

Accurate Risk Assessment

Bigger secrets require brain training and advanced mental strategies, just like critical data on a server requires an elaborate firewall. The most important step necessary to get better is an accurate awareness of your skeleton risk.

David Dunning, a professor of psychology at Cornell, has conducted a study of how we view others and ourselves in terms of morality. According to the study, we tend to gauge the morality of others more accurately, but we tend to greatly exaggerate our own moral strength as compared to actual practices.

We tend to think we would stop to help the stranded motorist more often than others. We tend to think we would help a little old lady cross the street more than others. If we found lost money, we would be more likely than others to turn it in. But Dunning's research shows we all tend to inflate our self-image and moral superiority.

In the same way, you can't just imagine you're better at keeping secrets. You can't imagine that you're more bullet proof than those idiots at work. You have to actually be better at hiding secrets than others are at finding them! You'll never get better if you're deluding yourself.

We understand that it's not easy keeping a secret safe for years or maybe even decades. You will often tire of the constant strain. You won't be able to unload your burden on your friends. You won't be appreciated for your ingenuity when you play this game like an all-star. So you have to dig deep as you keep your relationships safe and on the surface.

The secret to consistent improvement in skeleton security is brain training, which we will turn to in a moment after an important review.

How are you doing with the strategies and concepts we have set before you thus far? You must implement before you can improve. Are you being creative? Are you covering your bases? Are you embracing the fear of failure?

Try our Get Better Quiz as a check-up. If you don't ace this one, you better get serious about getting better.

The *Get Better* Quiz

Score each statement on a scale from 0 – 2, with 0 meaning "uhhhh…"
And 2 meaning "all over it."

1. **I meditate on The Skeleton Code fives time a day while facing east.** _____
2. **I have buried my secrets deeper than the Cold War bunker under the Capital.** _____

3. **I have at least three diversions and denials for each of my skeletons. ____**
4. **I have paid three people with significant gravitas who will validate my public persona if I have a closet breach. ____**
5. **For insurance purposes, I actively gather and catalogue dirt on the people most likely to expose my skeletons. ____**

Score Your Test by Adding Your Scores

8-10 points: You're in the skeleton zone!

4-7 points: Sketchy.

0-3 points: Buzzards are circling.

Beyond Your Automatic Brain

Making up your mind has a whole new meaning today. It's not easy to modify behavior, even when we are convinced it's a good idea. We have too many old and bad habits to overcome. When it comes to keeping secrets safe, it's important that you limit your mental risks, even as you expand your capacities.

The primary way to get better at protecting your priceless privacy is to move your efforts from the realm of automatic reactions to intentional processes. If you are a guard in the military, you must stay alert at all times with your "eyes peeled" and your ears on high alert. You must refrain from any activity that would distract you from your duty. Additionally, no person of any rank other than your commanding officer can countermand your orders.

When it comes to guarding your secrets, don't imagine the security guard at the museum who is half

You have to change the locks on that skeleton closet more often than you change your passwords.

asleep with his feet up on the desk. Think about the soldier patrolling the perimeter in a war zone. One is symbol and the other substance. You want the latter protecting your closet.

Don't be satisfied with hiding your secret and walking away. You have to get better at guarding. You have to change the locks on that skeleton closet more often than you change your passwords. You have to add a dead bolt or maybe a security system. For God's sake…these buried secrets want to get away, scare the stuff out of people, and ruin your life!!! Remember—hoot owls and skeleton keepers sleep with one eye open.

Which brings us to some important but disturbing neuroscience. It seems that our minds have a mind of their own. According to David Eagleman in his book *Incognito*, and Robert Burton in his book *On Being Certain*, our conscious minds are less in control of our deep and impulsive thoughts and feelings than we imagine. Much of our thought and action happens more like an airplane on autopilot than one being maneuvered manually. Our brains are always cooking and calculating below the surface—beyond our awareness.

These subconscious processes can and will sabotage your secret keeping. Your brain can unlock closets that need to stay locked—without asking for permission. If our brains decide we would be better off letting our skeletons get some fresh air and exercise, they can slip those closet doors open faster than your computer deals a hand of Solitaire. They can let your friends, enemies, and perfect strangers get a sneak peak inside while you're not looking. In short, our brains can, for their own purposes, engage in clandestine closet calamity!

The best way to minimize this risk is to be aware that your brain and your skeletons often share the same tendency toward reckless behavior. Because these subconscious tendencies are beyond our control, our best compensation is to maximize and develop the conscious capacities we share. That's where we turn our attention now.

Brain Training

We have suggested that Luminosity come up with an app to focus on skeleton security. Until they do, here are some non-digital insights gleaned from those who have studied the particulars of neuroscience— probably because they didn't have a real life. The idea here is to use these concepts to avoid mental pitfalls and take advantage of your capacities to pursue excellence in your action plans.

1. Repetition

There are many different theories regarding how the brain learns and becomes more efficient at mental and physical processes, but they all have some common features. The first and most important one is repetition. We learned this from the Department of Redundancy Department and from Daniel Coyle in *The Talent Code.*

Pro golfers like Jim Furyk and Jordan Spieth can hit a golf ball so consistently because they've done it thousands of times. Itzhak Pearlman can play scales in his sleep for the same reason. Practice doesn't make perfect, but it does improve consistency and speed. After many repetitions, hitting a golf ball or playing notes on a violin becomes an automatic activity that can be accomplished even under pressure.

What your brain can do while relaxed is inconsequential. Ask anyone whose secrets came out in a time of turmoil. You have to be better than that. Your goal must be a brain that can perform under pressure. Repetition is essential if you want to get better.

The same training is necessary for a concert pianist, master wood carver, or serious secret keeper. The individual neural impulses, with repetition, get bundled together and become highly efficient and almost effortless.

Coyle estimates that 10,000 repetitions can create a masterful and efficient neural pathway, whether you are hitting a tennis ball, throwing a clay pot, or keeping a secret buried. This kind of self-improvement is important no matter what strategy of The Skeleton Code you are following.

Why shouldn't you use this science to your advantage when your reputation, job, or new relationship is on the line? Since the brain is inclined to act without your permission, but is highly teachable, why not train it to keep your closet safe? Your brain can learn to perpetuate your persona even when you are under duress, which is when you need it most. Your brain can learn to deny and divert attention when the heat is on, but only if you've done the training. Remember, in this game it's get better or get caught.

Repetition is especially helpful when dressing for success. When asked about your life in social settings, you can be ready to spin a yarn that will elevate your brand, and it won't take 10,000 repetitions to perfect that elevator speech.

Repetitive training also works very well when you are practicing plausible deniability. A well-rehearsed explanation, like a well-rehearsed play, will please and satisfy your audience. A kneejerk excuse will summon a room full of tomato throwers. Yet, your brain needs more than repetition.

2. Closet Cross-Training

As every great athlete knows, getting into a workout rut brings diminishing returns. The worst exercise routine is the one you use over and over again. Everyone knows the value of a diversified portfolio, and every athlete knows the advantages of cross training, which helps develop and strengthen different muscles in different ways. If you want to keep getting better at keeping your skeletons at bay, you'll diversify your brain training.

Brain training for closet security always works better if you can combine it with other disciplines. This is the cross training principle. One can rehearse responses developed for plausible deniability, for instance, while on an elliptical machine at the gym. We enjoy ingraining features of our alter ego while doing the deep breathing exercises of yoga. Why just imagine the fear of being fried by exposure and shame when you can engrain the same emotion by watching chicken sizzle in a pan? Your brain thrives on these associations, so make them work for you.

Because you need to get better in defense of your closet as time goes by, why not merge your brain training with a complimentary discipline like judo, also a defensive art? Each body movement could be associated with a masterful diversionary tactic to protect your secret. The secret keeping tactic of fogging, for instance, is very consistent with the throwing technique in judo called Te-Waza.

Here's another example. Why not combine one of your offensive skeleton strategies with one of those graphic video games? Each time you blow away an enemy or a monster, recite a strategic Code phrase you're using to prop up your persona. It would go like this:

"Blam, blam, blam…Volunteer of the year."

"Pow, pow, pow…Most likely to succeed."

"Click, swish, kaboom…Employee of the month."

Use your imagination. The point is to combine your physical/mental training or game playing with your closet training because together they will take you to new levels.

Lillian had broken through more glass ceilings than she could count. She had broken into the male-dominated world of Air Force pilots. She had broken into the male world of commercial airline pilots, and she was in line to make captain.

Everything was going according to plan except for one thing: Lilli's personal life was in disarray. She had suffered a break up with a guy she thought might be the one, in part because her travel schedule and his travel schedule had caused too many problems. Both liked to be the mouse that played when the cat was away.

Get Better Or Get Caught | 137

Lillian had also been very close to her father who passed away the year before. Physically, she was in great shape, but she was noticing lapses in concentration, sleeplessness, and more fatigue than usual. She knew it was something short of depression, but didn't want to see it progress.

She decided to go see a doctor "off the radar." One can't be too honest about mental health, after all. That doctor prescribed an anti-depressant, and Lilli's symptoms improved quickly and significantly. OK, so maybe it was depression, but only a minor version.

As a female pilot, she simply had to keep this from her employer. It's difficult enough to advance in a man's occupation. She was doing fine on the meds and getting great performance reviews. She knew she was on track for that promotion and wasn't about to put it in jeopardy. Why would she risk years of experience and a great future when someone could over-react?

Lillian thought about seeing a therapist, but didn't want that expense out of pocket. She knew she needed to handle this matter herself. She bought some books on depression and mental health and began picking up phrases she could use during her medical exams and company interviews. She would practice these while she played Solitaire on her computer, repeating a phrase with every flip of the card:

"Losing my dad was tough, but I know he's proud of what I'm doing with my life."

"The breakup was hard, but it's better to get that stuff figured out before you get married. I don't need to be in a hurry to get into a relationship."

Being a pilot really helped Lillian get the most of her brain training. She was accustomed to following protocols and checklists, disciplines that translated easily into secret keeping. Her brain training techniques helped her better guard her secret, and she didn't get caught. But she did get that promotion. Remember to use your imagination.

Check Your Progress

Let's take a moment to review your progress in creating your own Code. Learning about skeleton security won't help you much if you don't put at least one plan into practice for each of the strategies we have named. If you haven't done it yet, choose at least one action plan in each of the major areas we have covered that can be your focus for improvement in the coming months. Why not address one of these each week and then repeat or devise another plan?

A Vital Note: If you write in this book, please keep it tucked away in that same secure closet where you keep your skeletons!

1. Dressing For Success: My action plan to improve in this area is

_____

2. Mimic The Masters: My action plan to improve in this area is

_____

3. Take The Offensive: My action plan to improve in this area is

_____

4. Personal Distraction: My action plan to improve in this area is

_____

5. Fear Failure: My action plan to improve in this area is

_____

6. Plausible Deniability: My action plan to improve in this area is

_____

7. One Way Trust: My action plan to improve in this area is

_____

As you begin to work on your plans to Get Better, be aware of your brain challenges and capacities. Your mind can be a terrible thing when it comes to closet security, but it can also be your best asset.

We close this chapter with the challenge of Churchill, who certainly had the fighting spirit of security: "Never, never, never give up." No matter what's in your closet; no matter how much those secrets try to sneak out; no matter how curious your friends and family are; never, never give up.

They say fish would never get caught if they kept their mouths shut. Well, you'll never get caught if you can keep your closet shut. If you're going to do that, you'll need a long-term commitment to excellence. It's really that simple: you have to get better at skeleton security or you'll suffer the consequences.

Chapter Nine

Come Out With Flare

Anything worth doing is worth overdoing.
—Mick Jagger

We hope you are finding success in your new skeleton security protocols, and we wish you many years of exposure-free bliss. However, we realize that some of you may decide to take another path. Maybe your closet will get too cluttered and chaotic over time. Maybe you'll just get tired of keeping watch over those secrets.

We hope our book will give you the power to persevere. However, if you ever make the decision to come out against our best recommendations, and to reveal what you have hidden for years, you should do it right. After all, you only get one chance to set those skeletons free, and like squeezed toothpaste, there's no going back.

A non-profit board was having its annual meeting and it was clear the organization needed a fresh new vision. Suddenly a genie appeared to them and offered to give the chairperson infinite wealth, wisdom, or beauty. She chose wisdom.

After the genie left, all the directors were looking at the chairperson whose face was glowing.

"Say something wise; give us your great insight," one of them said.

She looked at each one of them around the table, put her head in her hands and said, "I should have taken the money."

This chapter is about having a significant change of mind about your secrets and whether or not you want to keep them in your closet. We all know "the best way to ruin a secret is to tell it." However, we understand that you may get to a place of boredom, fatigue, or irritation and begin to think about what life would be like if those skeletons weren't taking up so much room in your house.

Typically, we all have these moments, but they usually pass and we find our way back to good security. We can never recommend "coming out," because it's more risky than keeping secrets. However, because a few will decide to set their skeletons free, we thought we should address the subject. If you're going to jump out of an airplane, you will need a good and well-packed parachute.

We're Here to Pump You Up

When it comes to outing your own secrets, whatever you do, don't whimper. Don't melt into the carpet. Don't fall apart or go into seclusion. This is the approach of weakness and will earn only scorn on top of humiliation.

Our research shows that you would be much better off coming out with flare. If it's worth doing, then do it with panache. Don't be half-hearted. Reach for the stars. Make it memorable. Name it and claim it. If you're going to fess up, come out like the celebrities at the Academy

Awards. Come out on the front page above the fold, not tucked away in the business section. Come out with guns blazing like Butch and Sundance (metaphorically). Come out with splendor, not sniveling.

Pull any book about business or personal success off the shelf and you'll find even more of these tantalizing clichés. Who are we to argue with such universal wisdom? Why not do the same if you finally decide to come out with your secrets? No matter how long your skeletons have had residence in your hiding places, when you decide to let them go free—when the locks come off and the closet doors are flung open wide (and again, we are not recommending this), you should create an exciting exposure plan worthy of a Silicon Valley startup.

Don't wake up one day and think, "Today's the day I tell everyone that I've been doing 10 additional shades of grey the book never mentioned." Don't walk out of the bar and text your advisor, "I've been using my scholarship money for Botox treatments." Stifle any of the usual "jerk" reactions, whether they happen in your knee or some other part of your anatomy.

Instead of over-focusing on the secret to be expunged, reframe the issue as beginning a new chapter of life. Who doesn't like new beginnings? Who doesn't celebrate and feel a little envy when someone starts a new business venture? Spin the outing of your secret as a turning point; a launchpad for the new you.

Brian figured he couldn't keep his sexual orientation a secret any longer. The double life was causing significant problems and he could not imagine how the truth could be any worse (believe us, the truth can always be worse). His friends who had come out started by telling their parents, but Brian knew this would cause a ripple effect of gossip and each wave would be a little juicier and more distorted. No, that was not going to do.

As an alternative, in order to better control the narrative, he considered launching a "coming out tour," with visits to all the significant people in his life, in a very short period of time. When he imagined repeating his story a hundred times, however, the idea began to feel like the proverbial Chinese water torture.

There had to be another way, and we suggested it to Brian using a unique Skeleton Code principle. We call it "exacterbation" and we coined the term to express a key strategy for coming out. "To exacterbate" is *to complicate or deteriorate a situation temporarily in a way that eventually leads to a strong sense of personal pleasure.* It requires some effort to be sure, but offers such sweet release in the end.

Brian invited his family and friends to a minor league baseball game to celebrate his birthday. At the end of the 4th inning, his entourage heard the announcer say, "let's all say happy birthday to Brian," and his picture suddenly appeared on the outfield mega screen. Then, on the same screen, Brian appeared via video and sang the following, to the Happy Birthday tune,

What a happy birthday,
And O by the way,
I'm having this party,
Just to tell you I'm gay.

The crowd applauded and cheered which drowned out the gasps and chokes from Brian's grandmother and father. As Brian's friends came to him to express their support, even his dad and grandma eventually joined in the mass celebration. Brian used the power of group dynamics to his advantage, and it worked like a charm. That's what we call flare!

Over years of study, we have discovered that a skeleton, like your face in the morning, is not ready for presentation to the public. Your secret may only need some exfoliation and two layers of Este Lauder: Other secrets need an extreme makeover that would make Joan Rivers proud (God rest her soul).

You should go ahead and assume that your skeleton is not ready for prime time, or any time. Almost every secret or discredited identity requires some refinement. If you decide to bring one out on stage, whether at the family picnic or on Entertainment Tonight, you'll need to be strategic about it. Think this through before you drink too much.

Beware the Accidental Way

There are three ways to come out of your skeleton closet with your skeletons in hand. There is the method of intentionality, which is the subject of this chapter—when people make a decision to out themselves. However, we should warn of two more disastrous ways that skeletons surface.

The second method, and least desirable way to vacate your closet, is to be exposed by another person. When people do not follow The Skeleton Code, this happens more often than you imagine. There is a vast hunger for good gossip, and many people you know are trying to keep that search engine online at all times. All is not lost, however. It is possible, even after being exposed by another, to employ some of the strategies in this chapter to mitigate the damage. You will have to act quickly.

There is a third way that skeletons are set free from their dungeons, and this method is both fascinating and tragic. It is the accidental way.

We regularly hear stories from people that involuntarily and unintentionally out themselves. This is different from the first method because these poor people fall victim to an unconscious process in their own brains that makes the exposure decision for them. It's a mental hit and run. This subconscious process often has the appearance of carelessness, though the brain never does anything by accident.

Trish, for instance, had become sexually active, something that would cause problems in her conservative family. Yet one day she left her birth control pills on her bathroom counter where her mother was sure to see them. This was not the action of a fastidious neat freak, which is what Trish was. Nor was it simple laziness or inattention. Rather, it was a subconscious request to let go of a secret.

We suspect that many high profile scandals fall into this subconscious category. When high-powered skeletons make too much noise for too long, their keepers often seem to self-destruct. They make mistakes far below their pay grade. It's almost like they leave breadcrumbs for the curious journalist or photographer.

We all remember the story of the infamous television minister who pumped up his crowd by zealously condemning sexual sin. Then, as it turns out, he had a preference for prostitutes himself. The same has been the case for those sworn to uphold the law: district attorneys, governors, police officers, and presidents. They not only make stupid decisions, they act out in ways that are destined to backfire.

While we always prefer tidy closets with skeletons all in a row, we recognize that some skeletons will never stay put. They will never sit quietly. They will rattle around until they find their way out because we don't have the right space to keep them, or we have too many prying eyes in our lives. You must be warned that some skeletons will eventually slip out with the key of your own subconscious and self-destructive machinations. The best thing you can do for these skeletons is to go out and find a really good lawyer and put him/her on retainer.

You may be skeptical that your own mind would open your closet door and set your skeletons free. Some mental health experts attribute this to our "anti-self;" our tendency to undermine our wellbeing. Not convinced? Read on.

We know that ineffectiveness is a Washington hallmark, but one must be reasonably savvy, image conscious, and paranoid to win and maintain a U.S. congressional or senate seat. Ordinary criminals are usually not playing with a full deck, which is why they get caught. Elected officials, on the other hand, typically come from a better criminality gene pool.

How can a male political figure of above average intelligence and successful experience intentionally text pictures of his bulging crotch to a female acquaintance? (Note: don't even send these to your own wife.) How can someone's faculties of reason fail so miserably that he would send lewd texts and emails to underage interns and pages? Or have a rendezvous in an airport bathroom? Or make regular appointments with high-end call girls?

We aren't making this up, you know! It happens with astonishing regularity, and these outings are only the tip of many icy cold closets. There are many more skeletons in Washington and Hollywood that are working their way into the light and will be coming soon to a media outlet near you.

When athletes and celebrities put their skeletons on stage, we are not surprised. After all, these people are known for their physical or acting prowess, not their mental prowess. Many have complexes or neuroses and don't feel any sense of social obligation to their public. We actually expect them to go out in flames, and would be disappointed if we suddenly had a dearth of falling stars and their mug shots.

But when those who live by a measure of public trust do the most inane things, one must conclude that there are mental and emotional processes at work beyond what most of us understand or care to imagine.

We know it's tempting to think that men lose their heads because they are thinking with the wrong one, but there's something bigger going on. How can a presidential candidate, for instance, make a sex tape with a lover…or a governor try to sell a senate appointment? There are gremlins running free in our minds, sabotaging our success.

On a gender awareness note, it may seem that men are more adept at this subconscious outing than women. They often rise to the highest levels of power and certainly have more testosterone. We should note, however, that men often have more opportunity than women to create sensational skeletons and to drink the heady wine of power. This wine, like Tequila, apparently makes your clothes fall off.

One of us, it must be said, does support the thesis that women in general are better suited for relational subterfuge. This may make them less likely to out themselves. Please don't interpret this as sexist. Maneuverability is a great asset if you aspire to live the Code. We know many women who are better skeleton managers than men.

Even so, many women who have realized great success in our society have engaged in behaviors that completely derailed or ended the careers they worked so hard to achieve. From Helen Chenoweth to Catherine the Great, women can do scandal just as well as their male counterparts, especially if they are from Alaska and like really nice clothes, or if they are running for president and want their dynasty back. There's more at work here than meets the eye or the mind. When our skeletons become too stressful, we are vulnerable to this process of being out-ed by our own subconscious sabotage. But it's a less than desirable way to come out. Better to have some control over the narrative.

Designing Your Press Release

So we've warned you about subconscious outing. There's really no security system that can protect you from your own internal hacking. So let's turn our thoughts to strategies we can control.

If you decide you no longer wish to keep their skeletons under wraps; if you decide to set your secrets free; you are much better off doing it well than sending a message from under a rock. These are our suggestions for Skeleton Confessions.

1. Come Out With Intention

Sometimes we get out-ed in uncontrollable ways, but we also have the right to choose! We know that people consciously release their skeletons for a variety of reasons. Some, for instance, know their secrets are going to come out and they simply want to get ahead of the inevitability to manage the process. Better to be a manager of the news than manhandled by the news.

Nicole thought she had finally found Mr. Right. Her relationship with Matt was going very well and she knew that "meet the parents" day would come eventually. For most women, this is an exciting step, but Nicole dreaded it. She lived far away from her father so none of her friends would meet him. You see, Nicole's dad had been a prominent leader in the Klan, and even though she despised his views, she also knew that guilt by association was the default posture for most people.

She knew she could not postpone "the meeting" indefinitely, so she decided it would be better to unlock her secret before Matt ever met her father. Her plan was nothing short of genius. She took Matt to the Civil Rights Museum in Birmingham, where they lived. This gave her an opportunity to tell him how strongly she supported equal rights and social justice.

When they stood before an exhibit on the Klan, she asked Matt what he thought about it. He said that he had a hard time believing such an organization could operate in this country for so long with virtual impunity. He did not understand how those people, many of whom were in places of social power and status, could be so hate-filled and violent. Matt told Nichole that he had experienced some pretty vile racial attitudes in his fraternity, but nothing like what he was seeing in the exhibit.

A tear rolled down Nicole's face as she looked at Matt. She said, "I'm afraid I saw this racial terrorism up close and personal."

"What do you mean?" Matt asked as he took her hands in his.

Nicole took out a tissue, dabbed her eyes, and said, "You've asked about my father and I've not wanted to talk about him. Do you know why?"

"No I don't," said Matt stroking Nicole's hair and trying to practice what he had learned in Active Listening class.

She turned and pointed to a picture in the exhibit. "Because the man in that photograph holding the shotgun…that's my father," she whispered.

And then she turned to Matt, who was stunned as he glared at the photo, and said (wait for it), "My father's racism is disgusting to me and I could never be with a man who was anything like that. Please tell me you aren't like that!"

We are in awe of Nicole's 360-degree slam-dunk. What finesse! What a maneuver. See, we told you women are better at this. Instead of mounting some defensive strategy, Nicole turned the tables. Rather than proving that she was not like her father, it was suddenly Matt who needed to be convincing. Instead of a secret that blew up in her face, her skeleton turned into a lovely dinner for two at her favorite restaurant while Matt assured her of his racial sensitivity.

To be sure, not every secret can be magically transformed from liability to asset like this, but with intention, some can. Learn from Nicole.

2. Cast Your Fate To The Wind

While we do not recommend this, some have survived an infamous and age-old method of dispatching secrets. They have cast their secrets and their fate to the wind and lived to tell about it. Others were not so fortunate.

This outing path is probably best suited for people with a terminal disease who are so tired of their secrets, they don't care how they come out or what it will cost. In fact, many "casters" secretly hope for a glorious demise, like the soldier running into enemy fire. If your future no longer matters to you, this could be an excellent exposure option. But choose very carefully. There's no going back.

A Texas rancher went to church one Sunday and the minister preached on confessing your sins. It was something the Bible said should be done. It was something that could be done with confidence in a place where everyone needed forgiveness. Then the preacher challenged the parishioners to stand and do just that—to confess their sins. No use holding back, he said.

A blue-haired lady up front stood and in a quivering voice said, "I've been gossiping all my life."

The minister replied, "Thank you for confessing that sister. God bless you."

A young man in the choir stood and said, "I cheated on my math test last week."

Again, the minister responded, "Thank you for that confession."

On and on it went, and the rancher was getting restless. He had a secret, but he wasn't ready to tell.

"I've held a grudge for years," said a woman in a blue dress.

"God bless you for that confession."

"I've had impure thoughts," said another.

"God bless you for that confession."

Finally that rancher sitting in the back thought to himself, "What the hell; maybe this is my moment to be set free." So he stood and said, "I've been having sex with my sheep."

And the minister said, "I don't reckon I'd have told that one."

Like we said, maybe you should be terminal before you choose this method. However, the advantage of "damn the torpedoes" is ease-of-use. It takes no planning. Simply take your hands off the wheel as you hurl down the interstate. That may be too graphic. Send a mass email. Put an ad in the paper. Tell old Ms. Johnson down the street and ask her not to tell anyone. Then, take a nap in your hammock and wait for the sky to fall. It's actually easier than 1, 2, 3—It's just a 1 and done.

We have been told there is some element of thrill when you cast your secrets out like this. Some say it's like raising your hands while you're on a roller coaster. Spraying your secrets can be a completely out-of-control gig, so if that's your buzz, go for it. Please do not, however, call us later and complain about the flushing sound that is your future going down the toilet.

3. Devise The Perfect Platform
If you decide it's time to spill the beans, the coffee, the milk, or whatever, it's preferable to choose your platform well, unlike the rancher. We have learned this lesson by watching people choose badly. Not every secret can be shared in any context.

If you must come out, choose your setting wisely. You have many options, including one with almost limitless possibilities: social media. Back in the day, only the rich and famous could make a tabloid splash. Now anyone can make a video and post it. You could rise from gutter to glory!

The advantage of well-made video exposure is that people get into the fun of it so much they forget to be shocked, disappointed, or upset. By well made, we don't mean professionally produced. We mean creative, interesting, over the top, and inviting. You need a great idea and some time, not money. Just browse YouTube and you'll find some ideas to get you started, and others that will stop you in your tracks.

If social media isn't your shtick, you have other up-close options with more history and a little less public exposure. In other words, if you want to come out to a smaller segment of the population, these ideas might suit you.

Our favorite skeleton unveilings have happened at family gatherings, holidays, or reunions. We counsel against workplace disclosures. Joyous or not so joyous family settings have the advantage of getting the word out to most or all of your significant others at the same time, thus avoiding any unnecessary embellishment or commentary that's inevitable when your story creeps through the family grapevine.

Marty came from a large family, and Thanksgiving was always a centerpiece of family life. No one missed that holiday get together for any reason short of death. Marty's parents had a large house with ample dinning space, so when Turkey Day came around, the table was lined with his four siblings, one sister-in-law, three grandparents, one aunt and uncle, and two cousins.

Marty's mother was the consummate hostess and cook. Her Thanksgiving table was legendary, and there was always enough food to feed the family three times over. And if the food was very good, the stories were even better, especially when Uncle Al had plenty to drink. There was no better time to catch up and entertain.

It was the perfect setting for Marty to come out. As desert was being devoured, he tapped his tea glass with a spoon to get everyone's attention. "I have something I need to tell everyone," he began, and then took another sip from his glass because his mouth was already dry.

"I know this rancher who has a special relationship with sheep" (just kidding). What he really said was, "I've been waiting until after grandpa was gone to tell you all this." Marty's mother sat down and with some panic in her voice said, "Well, don't leave us in suspense!"

You could have heard a feather float. "Mom, do you remember when we had that hyperactive dog Sparky that broke your really expensive vase from China? I remember how shocked we all were that you turned him in at the animal shelter, but I think we understood your feelings given the value of the vase.

"Well here's the thing. Grandpa and me were tossing the ball in the living room, being very safe, and there was an unfortunate bounce. That's what really happened to your vase. We panicked. We knew how much you loved that vase and knew you'd be really hurt. So we blamed Sparky, which seemed like a good idea at the time. We always blamed him when someone farted too. We didn't really think you'd take him to the shelter. I promised Grandpa I would never tell, at least as long as he was alive."

Marty's mother sat in stone silence for a moment and he had no idea what was going to happen. Then she just started laughing uncontrollably—the kind of laughter that almost makes you wet your pants. "I didn't like the dog anyway," she managed to say between guffaws. And then everyone else decided it was funny too.

Remember: the right setting matters!

4. Rumor Yourself

We have still another suggestion if you want to share your skeletons with panache and get your money's worth with *The Skeleton Code*. Why not start, and have some fun with, your own rumor about yourself? We know this can send a chill down your spine when you first hear it, but have an open mind. *Rumor* is such an ugly word when you're the object. But if you're going to open your closet, might as well open your creative options too.

Rumoring yourself is not unlike the trial balloon strategy in politics. It gives you a chance to test your messaging and tweak your spin. If you see that the rumor is going to send you down in flames, you can pull the plug on it yourself, since you started it.

The *rumoresque* strategy can also be helpful when you need to and want to soften what we call *skeleton shock*. Rumors can help others vent their feelings early before they

> Rumoring yourself is not unlike the trial balloon strategy in politics. It gives you a chance to test your messaging and tweak your spin.

hear the real thing. This is usually less traumatic for you and for those you hope will continue to be your friends.

To think of a good way to rumor yourself, first imagine that you are dressing up your skeletons for the party of a lifetime. When you find something that's stunning, or something that really fits with style, you'll be ready to pre-release an appropriate rumor into the pipeline.

Candace did a really good job with her "leak." She chose a very controlled rumor directed at her very conservative parents (from whom she had been most anxious to keep the secret). She enlisted her best friend, who was quite the actor, to do the job.

(Note: it is critical to start your rumor near the center of gravitas; with the person or persons whose reaction(s) you fear the most. This enables you to get the alpha version to them, knowing that down the line, the rumor will morph.)

This friend went to visit Candace's parents, Jerry and Mildred, and was very nervous and concerned. She told them she felt like Judas betraying her friend, but that she had to reach out for help. She had heard from very reliable sources that Candace was using drugs and maybe selling drugs, and that she was in partnership with some very troubling people. "I just don't know what to do for my friend," she cried. "I'm afraid to confront her. What if it's all a lie?"

As expected, the parents fell over themselves thanking the girl for coming to them. They promised to hold her name in confidence and to intervene in the best interest of their daughter. As soon as the friend left the house, she texted Candace: "Operation Relief In Process."

In about two minutes, Candace received an email from her mom, asking her to please come home after her class at the community college. Her heart began to race with eager anticipation.

When she walked through the back door, it was difficult to keep a straight face when she saw the grave expressions on her parents' faces as they tried to be calm and relaxed. She feigned surprise and concern when asked to sit down with both her parents, something that never happened. "Did somebody die?" she asked.

"We need to get right to the point," Jerry blurted. "Are you a drug dealer? Don't try to hide it if you are!"

"Settle down Jerry. This is our daughter," said Mildred. "Honey, I'm sorry, but we've heard a rumor that you are deeply involved with some dangerous people in the drug business. Is that true?"

Candace bowed and shook her head. "I'm so sorry I didn't tell you earlier," she replied. "I didn't want to worry or disappoint you. No, I'm not selling drugs. I was just going to a party with a friend and we had smoked a joint and we got pulled over by the police. He could smell it and we got arrested. There were no other drugs in the car, so we are going to have to do some community service, that's all."

"So you are not in the drug business?" her father asked.

"Of course not," Candace said. "You know how stuff gets blown out of proportion!"

"We are so relieved," said Mildred. "I mean I should probably be upset that you smoke that stuff. It isn't good for you, unless you're sick, I hear."

"You have every right to be angry," said Candace.

"O hell, how can I be angry?" said Jerry. "You just need to be more careful."

"I promise I will," said Candace. "Thanks for understanding and I'm really sorry to frighten you. I think the community service will be really good for me."

"Don't worry dear. It was such a little mistake," said Mildred as she announced her plans to take them all to the steakhouse.

We think it's a highly creative and effective strategy when you can humor yourself and rumor yourself at the same time. Good job, Candace.

Moving now from tactics to style points, let's consider some valuable ways to accessorize your outing. In some cases, this will make the difference between coming out with flare and going down in flames. There are actually several available options from which to choose, based on skeletal type and your own personal giftedness.

These are four ways to put some punctuation on your pronouncement, and to get the most out of your message. Even so, we understand that not every outing calls for grand drama. Sometimes, flare doesn't look like big and bold Broadway. Sometimes, it looks like a smooth getaway or a slight of hand that makes magic possible for your future. These next four techniques have just enough flare to keep you dancing another day.

5. Headline Your New Awareness

Many have found it very effective when revealing secrets to ensconce them in the language of new philosophical or religious awareness. This works better if you self-report your skeleton. Everyone gets philosophical or religious when they find themselves knee deep in scandalous alligators.

Katrina knew she was spending money she could never repay. Her credit card was maxed out and she often incurred penalties for late "minimum" payments. Her fiancé didn't know about her financial predicament. The two planned to buy a house when they got married, but Katrina knew the loan process would get derailed when her credit history was revealed.

She decided to come clean with her fiancé so he could get the home loan in his name. She used our new awareness tactic. It went like this:

"I'm very proud of your financial discipline, but need you to know that I've not managed my money as well as you have. In fact, over the years, I've built up some serious debt. I may need to file for bankruptcy or at least see a credit counselor for help.

"I've come to see that financial debt is like the slavery of sin we hear about in church. It imprisons me and keeps me from being all I can be.

I've confessed my sin to God and now to you. I hope you'll forgive me and help me live up to my new standards."

People may give you the benefit of newfound wisdom if you come clean before you get caught. If you want to try it, these examples will help you get started on your own version of enlightenment:

"I have told untruths and half-truths about people I don't like. I now see what a mockery I have made of their human dignity."

"We all learn from our mistakes, and I have made some. They have been effective teachers, however, and the best that I can do is take them to heart."

"I have been humbled by my weakness, and it makes me recall how judgmental I have been to others. Now, the grace of God is what I try to offer to others."

You get the idea.

6. Creative Contrition

This can be used along with new awareness, but is also its own strategy. We suggest not overusing it, however, given that it has been the broken record played at every public flogging for years. With overuse or poor use, it just heaps more scorn upon the fallen.

This is not usually the case when one is proactive with contrition; that is, when it accompanies your confession. One great thing about contrition is that it can be so easily embellished on the spot. Just about anyone can get into a believable "I'm sorry, I did it" feeling by channeling the feeling that you're sorry you got caught. Get in touch with the emotion of "I'm sorry I have to deal with this," or "I'm sorry I've carried this guilt around for so long," or "I'm sorry this is such a waste of time." Just be careful to vocalize the appropriate contrition.

As long as you appear sorry for what you did, it usually works. We suggest being more concise than you may be contrite. Going on and on undermines your credibility. For a good look at what not to do, we would refer you to videos and transcripts of some of the most overly contrite people on earth. Avoid their complex excuses, their agitated glares, and their look of general panic.

Governor Christie of New Jersey, for instance, was very sorry for the shut down of the George Washington Bridge, which caused all sorts of havoc in the area. His first mistake, however, was being sorry for two hours. No one is that sorry and everyone sees through it.

The governor was also sorry for what his underlings did and did not do. Doesn't help your cause. You can pretend to be contrite about someone else's failures, but you might as well be telling people how stupid you think they are. Everyone has a BS alarm that goes off when someone is covering their backside and bogus contrition sets off that alarm every time.

Other favorite and informative apologies that didn't work well have been offered by former President Bill Clinton, Governor Eliot Spitzer, golfer Tiger Woods, and cyclist Lance Armstrong. So many bad examples.

Think creatively. Bring flowers along with your new awareness. Sign up for the AA class so you can tell your boss the name, date, and time. Plan some act of atonement and complete it before your confession. This creative contrition along with your confession will serve you well.

7. Regret And Share Your Weakness

This approach to making your skeleton sharing less problematic is probably best used in conjunction with contrition, so as to avoid the appearance of blaming. The goal is not to avoid all responsibility for the thing you have said or done, but to share that responsibility so it spreads a little thinner. You must do this very carefully or it will sound like the classic childhood ploy: the blame game.

Remember—be circumspect rather than overly critical of your "bad influence." You are not only sorry for the thing you did, but also that you let someone else negatively influence you. While you have failed, the implication is that you would not have done so without the outside influence. This strategy also fits nicely into "new awareness." You will now be much more careful about going along with others when you have doubts.

Paul came into the office with a grade A hangover. He might have kept it from his boss if not for the presentation he had to give. Rather than wait to be discovered in the meeting, he decided to make a proactive trip to see the boss.

Knowing not to beat around the bush, he said, "Look Mr. Griffin, I have a splitting headache because I had too much to drink last night. I can do my presentation but it won't be as good, given how bad I feel. I'm really sorry. I should never have gone out with Billy over in maintenance. I think you probably know his reputation. I did too but thought I could manage. Clearly, I won't make that mistake again."

Admittedly, this technique works better if you are an adolescent or if you are under the influence of someone with more power or authority. These are expressions you can use in conjunction with clear contrition:

"I thought Cynthia was my friend and I trusted her. I should have known better than to accept her invitation to that party. I just don't need friends like that."

"I started smoking pot so early. By the time I was an adult, it had become too powerful an influence. I wish I had never met Frank. He was the really cool older guy in the neighborhood who gave me my first joint."

Do you see the balance between owning your issue and at the same time laying it at the feet of another? Likewise, you can often share the shame with a societal failure beyond your control, such as the sexual revolution.

8. Plus a Little Dessert

Here is one last example of subtle flare. If you want people to move beyond your scandal quickly, give them just a taste of something that might be sweeter or juicier. One cannot be too obvious with this deflection. Finger pointing is a sure sign of desperation and denial. So is fabrication, which will come back to bite you. Think of it as serving some dessert after you've eaten your crow.

What you want to do, in the context of confessing your secret, is to offer a well-placed passing comment about someone else that has or is struggling with the same or similar issue. This is not a lead in. It should follow contrition and new awareness. The comment needs to be true as far as it goes, but can also suggest the possibility of something more scandalous. It must be implication and not assassination.

Fred got his car insurance bill and the premium had gone up $1,100 because of his third speeding ticket. Knowing he could not keep this from his bookkeeping spouse, he decided to come clean.

"I got another ticket and the insurance has gone up," he blurted out over dinner. I'm sorry. I'll cancel my health club membership to cover it."

"What, so our medical bills will go up too?" said the wife.

"Well, I'll find something to give up since it's my fault. I really am sorry; I was late to that meeting. I guess it could be worse though. When I was at the courthouse trying to get the ticket reduced, I saw Bud and Karen going into domestic court. Can't imagine how much money that divorce is going to cost."

The purpose of this deflection is to help the other move past your problem quickly. After you have spilled your guts and groveled a bit, try something like this. Be sure to maintain the appearance of contrition and introspection.

"I am hopeful when I see couples like Bill and Barbara staying together… after all they've been through, and still may be going through according to some."

"As embarrassed as I am about my DUI, at least I was not an elder at the church. I guess you heard about that one."

"I hope the anger management classes are helpful. I obviously have some issues to deal with. When they decide to offer racist management classes, I'm going to register for two of my managers. Talk about over the line!"

You must be subtle. Use the velvet glove.

Remember, if you are going to come out, give yourself the chance to survive and maybe even thrive. Don't be halfhearted and don't be impulsive. Plan your outing like a picnic with your lover. Don't leave the process to chance. Rehearse your lines and imagine the reactions you'll get. Develop a contingency plan if your drama starts to veer southward.

Avoid excuses, excessive explanations, and blaming. Tout your new awareness and the hope you have for your future. Everyone loves a person who has overcome to find a new life.

Keep those secrets safe if you can, but if you decide to come out, use the ideas in this chapter and you'll have a story to tell! So will your friends.

Post-Satire

We have called the strategies in these first nine chapters, The Skeleton Code. We hope you have enjoyed their satirical nature. Now it's time to see them for what they are: stories and struggles that mirror the closeted nature of our lives—our chronic tendency to cover our weaknesses so that others will accept and love us.

It's tragic, really. To the degree we keep secrets, we also keep ourselves from being known and loved for who we are, which is the only authentic love we know of.

This book is not really about keeping secrets. It's about how crazy it is to live a duplicitous life. But we learn to live this way at an early age, and it's a hard habit to break. We therefore offer you a better way and hope that you'll keep reading the final two chapters we call The Skeleton Curse and The Skeleton Cure.

Chapter Ten

The Skeleton Curse

No man, for any considerable period, can wear one face
to himself and another to the multitude, without finally
getting bewildered as to which may be the true.
—Nathaniel Hawthorne

We hope that our satirical treatment of secret keeping in the previous chapters has playfully engaged your imagination. Yet the reality of hiding or denying the darker aspects of life is far from humorous. The great irony in keeping our skeletons tucked away, after all, is that we become the real and tragic prisoners in our proverbial closets.

In the second section of this book, we shift from satire to straight talk. First, in chapter ten, we will grapple with The Skeleton Curse. Keeping secrets always becomes toxic and we need to name and describe this. Toxicity shows up wearing many disguises. This chapter won't be easy reading. You may feel like you're watching someone make sausage, or replace a knee in surgery. But understanding the downside of skeleton maintenance is necessary motivation for choosing a different path.

Beyond this, we will shift to the final chapter we call The Skeleton Cure, and we hope that your perseverance in getting to this conclusion will be well worth the effort. There are ways to move beyond keeping secrets that become poisonous to our lives and relationships. No matter what's in your closet and how imprisoned you feel, you can move toward freedom.

The Downward Spiral

It has become painfully obvious to us, in our own experiences and observations, that wearing masks to cover personal weaknesses inevitably makes us victims of what we call the *Law of The Downward Spiral*. This law dictates that every lie requires at least a second. One deception or failure necessitates another to cover the first, and then a more elaborate one to cover the first two, and so on. Each secret requires more deception and the inevitable and illogical progression is downward, darker, and more destructive to our wellbeing. This deep dark dungeon becomes our prison and our curse.

If we are going to consider breaking free from the prison of our own closets, we will have to be honest about the real cost of keeping secrets. We will have to see that there are more negative consequences that come from keeping secrets than releasing them. In each of the negatives we discuss, however, are potential positives, so stay with us through the final chapter, as we also explore the benefits and strategies of transparency. In our final chapter, we will share some significant insights and techniques to find this freedom, and we hope you will take them to heart.

Everyone Has Skeletons

The impulse to hide from embarrassment or exposure is universal, and some would say archetypal, pictured in Adam and Eve hiding from God. Hiding from threats has also been hardwired into our brains since we roamed the earth with saber tooth tigers. That makes it a very old game.

When our identity and value as humans is based on the affirmation, acceptance, or adoration of others, our aversion to the shadowy parts of our lives becomes severe. We work harder and harder to appear like objects of envy rather than scuff-marked people from the second-hand store.

Because the failings of others give us a perverse pleasure of superiority, we assume that others will devour our forbidden thoughts and behaviors with the same enthusiasm. As the saying goes, "Weeds need no sowing and gossip no mandate." Instead of receiving understanding or empathy in our failure, we fear becoming the gossip du jour.

...there is nothing more common to humanity than deviation, no matter the norm. Human life is a universal mixture of good and bad. The line of demarcation runs right through every human heart.

It's all a sad and painful game based on a fig newton of our imagination (or figment). We think we will achieve happiness from others if they love us, but we are miserable in the pursuit. We fear rejection by others even as we practice a tragic form of self-rejection. In other words, our actions create the very reality we are trying to avoid.

Yet there is nothing more common to humanity than deviation, no matter the norm. Human life is a universal mixture of good and bad. The line of demarcation runs right through every human heart. Author Brené Brown has written clearly on this subject.

There are no unscarred lives. There are no pristine people. It is our nature to have thoughts that violate our own sense of morality because these thoughts and feelings are rooted in our subconscious. They may or may not have any relationship to present reality. Dark thoughts are common to human brain process, regardless of how upright you appear to your public.

Roughly half of all marriages end in divorce. You're not the only one who has wished your spouse would die. Most people think about ways to escape pain.

Too much religion is sectarian, tribal, and exclusive, so if you're carrying that kind of righteous judgment around, you probably inherited it. Everyone who embraces a religion begins that journey thinking they have to live up to some impossible standard.

If you "stretch the truth" to the breaking point, you are in good company. A 2002 study at the University of Massachusetts found that 60 percent of people lied at least once during a 10-minute conversation and told an average of two to three lies in that time. Truth-Benders belong to the largest fraternity in the world!

How can you meet someone for the first time and label him or her a jerk in less than a minute? Doesn't that mean you are a bad person? Actually, it simply means that something about them triggered something negative in your emotional memory. It could have been their voice, the way they laughed or their perfume. All of us experience these quick judgments, but we don't have to live in them or act on them.

Everyone is bothered by unwelcomed dark thoughts. Everyone has cut corners, given in to their lower instincts, or compromised their standards. Many feel significant guilt or shame for breaking taboos. Others enjoy the rebel role for a while and then live with the regret. This is our shared story.

We may all create secrets, but we don't all keep them hidden. Some people eventually give up the charade and toss their boney troublemakers out on the street.

Before we show you just how problematic it is to keep secrets, pause for a minute and take this inventory. Is your closet getting toxic? It might not seem so, but if these tendencies describe you, it may be past time for some spring-cleaning:

- Thinking about my skeleton interrupts my thoughts during the day;
- I imagine worst-case scenarios of being exposed for my secret;
- I modify my social agenda to protect myself from skeleton vulnerability;
- I experience life more negatively and am less sure of myself socially;
- I find myself to be more easily distracted in social settings;
- I have a more difficult time trusting other people;
- I have a strong desire to be in control at all times;
- I have grown more critical and judgmental of other people;
- I seem to have less capacity to adjust to new situations;
- I find it more difficult to concentrate;
- For no apparent reason, I can be overcome by guilt or shame;
- I sometimes feel that people know my secret even when that's improbable;
- I have dreams about being exposed or losing power;
- I am less likely to go out for social activities than I used to be.

If you checked more than one of these feelings, you may be living The Skeleton Curse. If you dare, keep reading to find out.

The Physical Toll

You may be thinking that your secrets, if they are causing any problems at all, could only affect your psychological wellness. Sadly, there's evidence that buried secrets can disrupt your physical health as well.

Humans often shun and bury difficult thoughts and feelings. Like a fever, troubling thoughts, feelings, and actions are indicative of inner struggles that often lie beneath our consciousness. They are like warning signals at a railroad crossing.

While it's mainstream to give a nod to the mind-body connection in medicine, we did not appreciate just how much influence personal conflict could have on our health until we had personal experience.

For years, a family member suffered from two chronic conditions: depression and sciatica. You might not be surprised about the connection between depression and repressed feelings. However, most of us would not have believed or understood a connection between pain and numbness in a leg and underground emotions.

This family member we'll call Lynn went to two neurosurgeons at renowned medical centers where she received the same diagnosis. She had a compressed disc in her lower back and bone spur material in the foramen that was causing pressure and pinched nerves going to her leg (this showed on the MRI but turned out to be a Red Herring).

Physical therapy helped very little, so the solution for both physicians was surgery. Lynn decided to see if she could endure. It was painful and seriously affected the quality of her life. She could not sit for long. She had to give up tennis. She took too many pain relievers. When the pain was on, it was a big distraction.

Sitting with her sister at a restaurant in Raleigh, in significant pain, she complained about her dilemma.

Her sister said, "I have a book you need to read. It's called *Healing Back Pain* by Dr. John Sarno."

"What's it about?" Lynn asked.

Her sister, with a gift for directness, said, "It's about figuring out 'who' you'd like to kill!"

Two things then happened simultaneously to Lynn. First, her pain stopped. When she tells the story, she always says, "I kid you not…it went away completely just like that" (as she snaps her fingers). Up until that time, her pain had never just stopped. But it did—completely.

The second thing that happened as quickly as the pain stopped is that Lynn thought about her spouse. As bad as her marriage was, she had never consciously thought about wanting to kill her husband. As she would find out later, the real anger she was repressing was self directed and only mirrored in the spouse, as is usually the case.

Because her sister's question about "who' you'd like to kill" was so off the wall, the repressed feeling of anger slipped up into her awareness. Lynn was sitting on a truckload of rage…at her spouse and at herself for living in such brokenness. When the repressed emotion came out, the symptom of her repressed emotion (sciatica) went away.

Initially, we figured Lynn's relief must be some kind of placebo effect, but as we've read more about it, we think perhaps it was the pain, and not the cure, that was the real phantom. Her pain was VERY physical, but it had an emotional cause. That seems odd to those of us weaned on Western philosophy and medicine.

Our brain's propensity to keep secrets from us and to repress difficult thoughts and feelings is probably a survival instinct—a system of defense. Rather than being inundated and distracted by emotions, this mental management enables us to function in spite of powerful feelings that could overwhelm us. Yet this repressing tendency has too many negative side effects to make it an unqualified asset.

We could mention other connections between repressed secrets and physical health, such as depression's symptomology, but others have written well on the subject. Even if you are skeptical about the mind-body connection, we encourage you to look more closely at the subject. Your secrets could be causing physical problems.

Secrets Are A Drag

We don't think it's healthy to marinate in feelings of guilt or shame or to continue to live a secret life as if that's a solution with no cost involved. Having a dark side isn't the problem. Hiding from it is. Doing or thinking things that would harm your reputation is not the greater risk. Pretending these things can be closeted without paying a high price is. Keeping secrets is a drag, a big drag.

One summer, on Lake Isabella east of Bakersfield California, a family had just launched their brand new boat. The day was beautiful but their 22 ft. Bayliner was acting sluggish. It just wouldn't take off. The "captain" tried everything he could to figure out the problem. He even pulled out and read the owner's manual. The engine seemed to be running fine, but it was like the boat was in mud instead of water.

Finally, he made his way to a nearby marina…slowly. A mechanic checked the engine and the movement of the outdrive, and everything seemed to be working fine. So he sent one of his workers over the side to check under the boat. The worker soon came up choking on water, he was laughing so hard. "I think I found the problem," he said as he pulled himself out of the water. You see, under the boat, still strapped in place, was the trailer.

Secrets are a drag on your life. Sure, you can keep those skeletons hidden for a time. They won't start their rattling rancor right away. But pushing them to the back of your mind, trying to ignore them, or attempting to cover them will take its toll. Eventually, the cover-up work becomes more problematic than the fear or reality of discovery. Until you bring those secrets to the light of day, they will turn nasty in your priceless mind.

Chances are if you keep your secrets in any of the ways we have satirically described, you will drive yourself crazy or worse. There has been significant research on the impact of burying (repressing and suppressing) thoughts or emotions. All of it tends to support only one conclusion: it's a very poor life strategy, especially in the long term.

There was a television show back in the black and white analog era called *I've Got A Secret*. It was a bit like a game show where guests appeared before a four-person panel. These guests had done something, or had some skill, that was highly unusual. By asking questions, the panelists tried to discover the guest's secret, and each incorrect guess by a panelist put a whopping $5 in the guest's pocket. They could earn as much as $80 for an appearance. The show was on the air for more than a decade because we all loved, and still love, to uncover secrets—almost as much as we love passing them along.

When it comes to our own secrets, however, this game is no game at all. There is no amusement about our own closets. There is no prize for keeping up appearances. We know this is troubling, but it's also reality.

Secrets Are A Brain Drain

There was an interesting study done by Kurt Lewin on memory that involved men and women who waited tables. It seems that they had very good recall about what their patrons ordered until the check was paid. After that closure, they could no longer call up the information in their minds. It's now called The Zeigarnik Effect.

One of the supported hypotheses of the study related to working memory in our brains. Our brains keep information in these systems like we might keep a file on top of our desk because we know we'll need it frequently. We keep it close at hand. Eventually, when that "case" is closed, the file goes off the desk and into a cabinet. Our brains do something like that when a mental process is "concluded" and no longer needed at our fingertips.

Yet this conclusion never happens with secrets. They can never be put away because they are ongoing issues. Keeping a secret safe is an active mental process. It is quite the opposite of closure. Therefore, the brain keeps the protective processes "running in the background," even though we want these files buried in the back of a file cabinet. Even when we're not thinking about them, they are cluttering our mental desks.

Hiding secrets prevents closure, which means our brains keep working on some solution, even when we are not aware that we're burning the mental energy. And the solution, almost always, is not to reverse the thought, erase the taboo, or atone for the sin. The solution to a secret, and its primal power to keep us broiled in conflict, is to release it in a responsible way.

Secrets, including those we keep from ourselves, burn enormous brainpower. Do you find yourself easily distracted? Have your powers of concentration declined? Do you make silly mistakes even when you are trying to take care? All of these symptoms could be the result of energy you are expending on keeping that closet secure.

Secrets distract us from living, like the loud party upstairs keeps us from sleep. They drain our energy like leaving the headlights on when the car is not running. And they will do this until we find the closure of openness. Our secrets need to find some light, even if it's in the privacy of a doctor's office.

The Problem of Projection

The mental process called *projection* is ubiquitous, though it operates below our radar. Projection is an unintentional seeing and sensing of our own issues or emotions "in" other people. We think we are observing something about Jack or Jen when in reality we are observing our own stuff being reflected back to us in their actions. Projection focuses on the external as a means of escaping the real pain that is internal.

This subconscious process is difficult for most of us to accept given our assumption that we naturally perceive what is true about our external reality. We would only ask you to consider that projection may in fact be distorting your emotional reality because of what you have locked up in your closet.

Ken's daughter Kristen began to show symptoms of a serious mental illness when she was fourteen. Over a period of eight years, she had five psychotic breakdowns, two of which required hospitalization, and each of which caused some brain damage. He was terrified, horrified, and mystified by the experiences and also troubled that "modern medicine" could do so little to help. The lock-down psychiatric unit felt like a physical and emotional prison. Kristen's decent into a life limited by mental illness was matched by his own decent into depression. For years, it seemed that he was experiencing his daughter's pain, struggle, and loss. It was the worst time of his life.

Years later, when a friend of Kristen's had to be hospitalized with a similar illness, he asked what she remembered about her earlier experience in the hospital. She thought for a moment and said, "The food wasn't very good." They both laughed until they cried. The memory of those experiences was still very real to Ken, but not nearly as troublesome for Kristen. Most of his pain was projected.

Thankfully, after years of therapy, Ken has discovered that the pain he was feeling "for his daughter" was his own, not hers. She was negotiating her illness with much more resilience than he was, though he could not see that through his own pain. The reason he thought she was suffering badly was this mental reversal called projection. He was projecting his suffering onto her.

No one has to teach us how to do this. We seem to be hardwired with an innate tendency to pin our own issues, including our faults or failures, onto others, even if that identification is a complete fabrication. It's not about them. When we cannot manage our own angst, or when our thoughts and feelings are buried, we seem to be compelled toward slinging mud on others who may be dealing with the same things.

Scapegoating is a common expression of projecting, and it gets more acute when we are keeping skeletons.

Projection is like mental slight of hand. It's a subconscious brain activity that "paints" our issues onto other people or situations as a diversion from the dark reality in our own lives that is too frightening to deal with, like secrets. It does this below our radar of realization. That's why you have a difficult time believing that it's happening.

To explore this further, we recommend the insights of Byron Katie, which can be found at www.thework.com. There you will learn that your secrets and your problems with other people are basically a problem with your own sense of reality. Our projections are images and thoughts created in our own minds, not coming to us from some external reality.

As Byron Katie suggests, our minds often sense what is right, but get it backwards. Many of the negative thoughts we have about other people are true insights, but not about them. They are about us. Other people simply function like a powerful mirror in which we see something true about own lives, if we dare recognize it as such.

The disrespect you feel in your marriage—that you think is coming from your spouse—is not a delusion, but it's probably not coming from your spouse as much as it feels. The greater issue is almost certainly your own lack of self-respect. When you don't respect yourself, even the smallest slight by a spouse (or another) will trigger the same emotions that are already assaulting your own sense of worth.

The lack of trust you see in your co-workers may be a real issue, but you're also likely seeing your own trust issues reflected back to you. When you feel these powerful emotions that seem to be triggered by others, step back and do as Byron Katie suggests. Turn the offense around to see if it might be truer about you. Maybe it's true that "Marsha doesn't trust me," but it might be truer that "I don't trust me," or "I don't trust Marsha."

This same dynamic is at work when we keep secrets. As long as they stay unexamined and unchallenged, in the dark and out of sight, we will continue to see them mirrored in others and never find healing within ourselves, which is where we need to look. This is yet another way that secrets poison our lives and stunt our growth.

Fear as Fantasy

Most chronic fears are products of our complex mental processes rather than innate responses to actual threats like walking through rattlesnake country or hearing a tornado siren go off in Oklahoma. They are emotions that accompany the stories we create about our lives. Our minds are genius when it comes to imagining what could go wrong in the future, even if we're sipping a mint julep on the front porch of our beach house on a clear summer day.

The fear we experience about our secrets can be overwhelming and debilitating. It also tends to be over the top. We imagine the worst-case scenario. We see ourselves humiliated for the rest of our lives. We see our friends running for the exits like there's a fire in the building. We see ourselves alone in our den at Christmas with pizza boxes everywhere watching *The Fault In Our Stars*. It sends shivers down our spines.

Americans love horror movies and we are constantly writing these horrific scripts about our secrets getting out; how our lives will be ruined, how much we will suffer, and how embarrassed we will be. This is our rut when we embrace rather than question our fears, most of which are rooted in fantasy.

When Janis was a student of dance therapy at New York University, she did her internship at Bellevue Hospital, on the locked psychiatric ward. After she held her first session, which was quite successful, she hurried to leave the ward to get to class. She went up to a staff member and asked to be let out. He looked at her with a slightly surprised smile and asked, "What do you mean? I'm not going to let you out."

Janis was a little bewildered by his answer, but tried to explain. "I'm a student at NYU and have to get to class. I've just been here to lead a session. Look, here are my notes. Can you please let me out?"

He laughed incredulously. "Yeah right. And I'm a student at Harvard. I can't let you out."

Janis suddenly realized she was stuck in a locked ward, and that anything she said would not be believed. Her pleas would be thrown right back at her. She was locked in the staff member's concept of her as a patient. She tried to reason with him for a few more minutes, but to no avail. She felt anxious and trapped. Everything she said to the guard just plunged her deeper into the chaos.

Finally, she decided to turn back and look for her supervisor, the doctor in charge. She eventually found him and told him what had happened, pointing to the staffer. The doctor looked at her while suppressing a smile and asked, "Janis, why are you asking a patient to let you out?"

When we are trying to keep our skeletons locked away in their own asylum, we often fall victim to the fantasies of fear. We live lives of secret desperation; afraid that who we are won't measure up; that what we are won't be accepted; that how we live or dress will bring derision; or that whom we choose to love will be the object of rejection and ridicule.

This fear becomes acute when we break a taboo. We make a mistake. We have an issue and we hide it, like humans have done from the beginning of time. Then the fear becomes chronic. We begin to cover our tracks and erase our fingerprints. We clear our browser history and erase our phone records. We may feel some relief when it seems we have locked that skeleton away. Yet we soon discover that our fear won't stay in a closet. It roams and disrupts our lives at will. It becomes a stalker, always moving in the shadows and in the darkness.

In Summary

It is clear that keeping secrets from others or from yourself is a hazardous approach to life. We have tried to overstate the case because most of us overestimate our coping capacities.

Cynthia resisted online dating for over a year, but finally decided to create her "profile." As is often the case, she created an idealized version of herself. She loved books she'd never actually read. She traveled to places she had only seen in guidebooks. She completed graduate work she had only planned, and held the job she dreamed of having one day.

There are only two ways such a story can play out. First, one might never meet another person attracted to the profile. But even worse, one could connect with a very nice someone online but never get to build a relationship with that person because of the phony profile. Either way, it's a dead-end.

We may not be able to keep ourselves from creating secrets, but we don't have to keep hiding the ones we create. Before we turn to The Skeleton Cure, here's a recap of reasons you might want to collect stamps instead of skeletons.

- **Sharing a Cell With Your Secrets**. To lock up secrets is to imprison part of yourself in the process.
- **The Downward Spiral.** Covering secrets often entails cutting corners, which in turn creates additional secrets that need to be covered.
- **Hiding From The Hiders**. Foibles, failures, and fantasies are universal, which means we are always hiding them from people who are hiding something like them.
- **Your Body Can Pay The Price Too**. Buried and repressed thoughts and feelings can present themselves in physical symptoms that significantly compromise wellness.

- **Wasted Emotional Energy.** We divert enormous amounts of energy away from healthy living in order to maintain skeleton closets.
- **Brain Running in the Background.** Hiding our secrets from others does not stop them from being "managed in the background" like a hidden computer program.
- **Projecting Problems.** Suppressed and repressed secrets make us prone to projection and using others as scapegoats.
- **Fear Worse Than Reality.** The fear of having secrets exposed can be more fantasy than reality.

A Final Image

Before moving to our final chapter, The Skeleton Cure, consider this challenge from Dr. Martin Luther King, Jr., from his 1967 sermon *But, If Not*, delivered at Ebenezer Baptist Church. His words are on target for the challenge of integrity before us.

> *"You may be 38 years old, as I happen to be. And one day, some great opportunity stands before you and calls you to stand up for some great principle, some great issue, some great cause. And you refuse to do it because you are afraid… You refuse to do it because you want to live longer. You're afraid that you will lose your job, or you are afraid that you will be criticized or that you will lose your popularity, or you are afraid that someone will stab you, or shoot at you or bomb your house; so you refuse to take the stand. Well you may go on and live until you are 90, but you're just as dead at 38 as you would be at 90. And the cessation of breathing in your life is but the belated announcement of an earlier death of the spirit."*

The great opportunity we are addressing here is called being completely honest about your life. The prospect can be frightening. Not only might you be criticized or marginalized by some, you might be "stabbed in the back." You might be shot with insults and judgment. The life you are trying so hard to keep together might explode into a million fragments, or so it seems.

So you may be tempted to keep those secrets, no matter the curse. You may think that this choice will be a better way to live, but giving in to the fear is just a pathetic way of dying before you die.

Reject the path of fear and stand up for the great principle of being true to yourself and others. Your freedom from fear is a path nearer than you realize. It is a path of outing your secrets and embracing your intrinsic worth. Freedom is a path of learning great lessons from your secrets and allowing them to reveal the treasure of your soul. We call that path The Skeleton Cure.

Chapter Eleven

The Skeleton Cure

If you tell the truth, you don't have to remember anything.
—Mark Twain

If you are ready to move beyond The Curse toward The Cure, let's begin by imagining what your life would be like if you no longer had to drag your secret around like a ball and chain. Imagine not having to keep up appearances at work. Imagine being completely relaxed around your family and friends. Imagine not having to remember your cover-ups, deceptions, exaggerations, or excuses. Imagine loving and accepting the real you, including your weaknesses. Imagine the friendship of others who actually know you and maybe even like you because you're "flawed" like them. We want you to know that this freedom is better than you can imagine.

But how do we find our way to this new open closet freedom? It can't be an easy journey or everyone would do it. On the other hand, it must be possible because so many have found their way.

Christopher Columbus returned to Spain from his voyage to the New World and became quite a hero. At a dinner given in his honor by the Cardinal, Columbus was surrounded by the best and the brightest minds in the kingdom. All were eager to learn about his exploits…except for one that was growing more exasperated by the minute, envious of all the attention that was going to Columbus. Finally he blurted out something like, "It was only a matter of time until someone discovered this new world and anyone could have done it."

Maintaining his composure, Columbus took a hard boiled egg from a platter and asked if anyone present could balance it on its end. The astronomer tried. The musician tried. The man of medicine tried. They all tried including the scientist who had given the challenge. No one could balance the egg on its end.

Laughing, Columbus took the egg, tapped one end of it on the table until the shell crumbled just a bit and let it stand there in balance. He looked at the other great minds around the table and said, "It always seems like anyone can do it after someone shows you how."

Anyone can find the new world of personal integrity and transparency because others have been there and can point the way. We have heard their stories and lived ones of our own. You can find this new life too, but it won't be easy getting past the habits of guarding, protecting, covering, and diverting. When you discover this freedom, however, you'll never again submit yourself to secret slavery.

Anyone can find the new world of personal integrity and transparency because others have been there and can point the way.

A Compass, Not A GPS

Many books in the self-help genre focus on practical, step-by-step actions to help readers achieve goals. This works well when the subject is starting a business, losing 20 pounds, or making something like a chocolate soufflé. Yet not every aspect of human progress can be reduced to a recipe. Our psyche is not a machine, nor is mental and emotional health the result of following a very good checklist.

Learning to be honest with others and with yourself is more art than mechanics; more feel than formula. We are addressing personal vulnerability here, not a home DIY project. One can learn to apply oil to canvass in a pleasing way with help, patience, and practice. Yet one never learns to create art by using a paint-by-numbers set. Lines and numbers are simpler to be sure, but immensely less satisfying. That's why The Cure isn't "fold tab A into slot B and then repeat with C and D."

The Cure is a journey toward new personal insight and openness, not a destination of ultimate arrival. It is a long journey most people don't begin until midlife when they start to take inventory of their lives. It is not like any other trip we make in life.

We have all grown accustomed to using GPS when we travel to new places. We like entering an address and having a pleasant voice direct us as we make every turn along the route until we have reached our destination. Even when we get off course, the program will recalculate to help us find our way. Yet there are no such guidance systems for the journey toward the freedom of deep honesty.

Finding our way on this trip is more like the ancient practice of using a compass. A compass won't take you to an address or define your every step, but will keep you headed in a specific direction. If you wanted to travel south, for instance, through unfamiliar territory, you would hold the compass level and steady and note the direction of the needle pointing north. Then, you would face in the opposite direction (south), look up and find a distant object on that visual line, put the compass back in your pocket and make your way to that distant reference point. Upon reaching the rock outcropping or cluster of trees, the compass would come out again and the same process would be repeated.

This is how we make our way along the path of freedom and wholeness. We know we want to move in the direction of greater transparency. We know we want to grow into full acceptance of our reality and ourselves. There are no GPS directions available, but there are markers and reference points in the distance that will lead us in the right direction. As we make our way to these, others will come into view that keep us on course.

In this chapter, we are going to identify several markers that lead in the direction of personal freedom and healing. You will have to make your own way toward these reference points because it's *your* journey. If you get off course, these markers can always redirect you.

The Cure is a lifelong journey, but one that enhances your quality of life all along the way. The further you go, the freer you become. If you're ready to start the journey, let us first tell you the direction we're headed. Then we will define those markers or reference points that will be our guides.

First, we are going to challenge you to aim toward deep honesty with others. To do this, you will have to open your closet and bring your skeletons into the light at some level. Moving in this direction will create some fear, whether you sense it or not. Your mind will create a hundred reasons not to go down that road, but you must. Vulnerability isn't the only path of life, but you can't get to wholeness without it.

Second, we want to direct you toward deep honesty with yourself. This will be an inward journey toward your True Self, the source of your ultimate value and resilience in the face of struggle and failure. You may not know or understand this concept, but we'll describe it later. If you have been hiding skeletons, you probably have never met this "real you," so we will make the introduction.

The adventure toward deep honesty with others and with self is NOT two journeys but ONE, even though we will separate them here for discussion. Again, this path cannot be charted with satellites or maps because our lives are too varied and complex. There are markers, however, that will point you in the right direction.

Marker 1: Reality Check

The Cure has to begin by moving toward self-honesty. This book has been about keeping secrets from others, but you are just as likely to be keeping secrets from yourself. You may be completely unaware of this. At AA, they say, "You are only as sick as your secrets," and they are talking about self-deception most of all.

The key to honesty with others, Shakespeare expressed through one of his characters, is "to thine own self be true." Before we can get real with others, we'll need to get brutally honest with ourselves. Our propensity for rationalization is limitless. Our willful blindness is epidemic.

Before we get to honesty with others, we will have to revise the narratives we have created for our own protection. These are often "lies" we tell ourselves to reduce our feelings of guilt, or the spin we put on our stories to take the edges off. Don't assume that the way you think about your skeletons is free of embellishment. It will be of little value to release a skeleton you have dressed up beyond recognition. Try this exercise:

Write out your secret the way you've dressed it up to be less offensive, then strip away all the old coats of paint and varnish you've put on it over the years, and express the raw truth about it in the least sensitive way possible (this is for your eyes). Then give a brief bullet list of how you respond to that skeleton reality. It might look like this.

Dressed Up Version: *One night, I saw someone who looked like my father kissing another women in a dark parking lot; I could have been mistaken and didn't want to accuse anyone if I wasn't completely sure, so I dropped it.*

Undressed Version: *I saw my father kissing another woman in a dark parking lot. I didn't want to believe it, but I also recognized his car. I never said anything about it to anyone because it upset me so much.*

- This has poisoned my relationship with Dad and he doesn't know why;
- I could never decide if I should tell my mother so I didn't and now I feel overwhelming guilt;
- I didn't want to be the reason my parents divorced but they don't have a marriage anyway. And I don't have a real relationship with either one;
- I feel intense anger at everyone involved, including myself.

Before you check your skeletons out of the closet, as we will discuss in a moment, try this reality check. *The only way to freedom is to release the unedited version of your secret, not the domestic one you've been living with.*

Marker 2: Face Your Fears

You must not only recognize but also move toward your fear. Moving in the direction of deep honesty with others and toward the first experience of sharing your secret will be a test of courage. You will have to face your fears.

Fear will be the devil on your shoulder telling you to put more locks on your closet. Fear will bargain with you to maintain the secret status quo. Fear will tell you the risk isn't worth it; that all hell is going to break loose if you let those skeletons go free.

The path to honesty will be uphill, yes, but will reveal ever-expanding vistas in the process. If you're not facing some fear on this journey, you're not facing the right direction.

C.S. Lewis described this universal human phenomenon: Everyone wants to get well, but no one wants to go to the doctor. Even though we might get well, we might also get something we don't want in the process. Ed Friedman echoed this when he wrote, "There is no way out of a chronically painful condition except by being willing to go through a temporarily more acutely painful phase." Sharing our secrets is not nearly as difficult as we imagine, but walking through the fear is no easy task. However, it is the only way.

Gordon Dalby tells about a man who was troubled by a recurring dream. In this dream, a ferocious lion was chasing him. The dream would end when the man would collapse in exhaustion, and he would wake up screaming.

The man was invited to relive the dream as he met with his therapist. When the man was able to visualize his enemy approaching, the counselor said to him, "When the lion approaches, do not run but instead, stand there and ask him who or what he is and what he is doing in your life."

The man shifted uneasily in his chair and then said, "The lion is before me, snorting and shaking his head. Then he asked, "Who are you and what do you want?"

After a moment of quiet, he opened his eyes and looked at the therapist. "When I asked him, the Lion replied, 'I am your courage and your strength. Why are you running away from me?'"

Your fear is another marker on the road to freedom. Turn and face those fears. Walk to them and through them because that which frightens you also holds the key to your courage and freedom.

Marker 3: The Trusted First

To continue the journey toward honesty and freedom, you will have to share your secret with the right person. This coming out experience will feel a bit like skydiving.

When Ken was younger, he flew a jump plane for a local parachute club. His saying was, "Why would anyone want to jump out of a perfectly good airplane?" Yet some people did and still do! Everyone who jumps from a plane must overcome some level of fear the first time they do it. Also, they would never do it if they did not have a significant level of confidence in their primary and emergency chutes. These silk saviors are packed with the utmost care.

Pulling a skeleton out of the closet for the first time requires a leap of courage and should be done with care. Your aim is to speak openly and honestly about your secret with the right person or persons. We don't know who needs to hear and respond to your secret, but it's almost always best to begin that jump into vulnerability with someone who is trained and prepared. Someone has to be the first to hear.

Back to the metaphor of skydiving... You have probably seen pictures of beginner parachutists doing what is called a tandem jump. This method pairs a jumping expert with a beginner. The two are literally bound together with the beginner in front and the expert behind. The experienced jumper gives courage to the novice as the two leap out of the airplane together. The pro brings balance and control to the free-fall so that the beginner's fear gives way to exhilaration. And, of course, the seasoned skydiver ensures the opening of the chute at the proper time and a safe landing for both.

Why take the fearful jump of telling your secret without the benefit of someone who has done it a thousand times and understands the process? Whether therapist, minister, or counselor, these skilled listeners are bound by rules of confidentiality. Their offices are safe places to set your secrets free. But here's the best part: They've already heard it all and probably worse. They know your public persona is fiction. They realize every person is a mixed bag. No matter your secret, they will listen and understand.

We don't know what your secret is, but we know it's not unique. Your therapist will not go screaming out of the room when you tell them about your fantasies or indiscretions, nor will they judge you, lecture you, or otherwise devalue you. They are not Olympic judges that score your performance in life, nor do they make recommendations to God about your eternal destiny. They are simply very good listeners, or at least most of them are.

There is someone near you who holds a key that will begin to release you from the prison you created to guard your secrets. That freedom will be worth any cost you have to pay, though most insurance plans have very reasonable short-term benefits for therapy. Find that qualified person. Set up an appointment and jump.

Don't waste a professional's time or your own when you meet. Prepare your explanation about why you are there and get right to it using the checklist below. Don't put it off by giving your life history. The sooner the words come out of your mouth, the sooner you'll be free-falling toward freedom. Until you find a way to speak about your secrets to another, they will be a chasm between you and wholeness. Speaking honestly, on the other hand, becomes the bridge.

Plan Your First Jump Checklist

Before we move to Marker 4, let us help you prepare to make that first jump into secret sharing. Use this checklist to get ready for that key conversation. Write out your recollections and thoughts about the following list. It's an important step to transfer your thoughts from heart to paper. This will help you transfer them verbally when you take that first step with your counselor or confidant.

- Remember your earliest experiences with your secret and how it came to be;

- If someone in your family in the previous two generations struggled with the same issue, briefly tell that story. This may require some sensitive investigation;
- Recall the influences that surrounded you and the context out of which your secret emerged; the purpose is not to make excuses but to expand your awareness;
- Who has been hurt because of your secret? Name the person(s) and what your secret did to them;
- What was missing in your life that led you to engage in your secret? Own this;
- How has your secret diminished your life? Be brutally honest here;
- How would your life be different if you no longer had to keep your secret? How would it impact your family, your work, and your self-esteem?
- What has this secret taught you about life? Look beyond the quick cynical answer to find the one that will open your eyes to something profound. Look for the answer that stirs your heart;
- What would you like to hear from the person to whom you have revealed your secret? Tell them about this need.
- If you believe in a Higher Power, ask for help and guidance, not to become fault free, but to become secret free and open to new awareness.

Once you have put your thoughts on paper, you will have a narrative to share with your counselor, trusted friend, or other confessor. It will also help you shape a much simpler letter that might be sent to someone who was or is impacted because of your secret. We will address that at Marker 5.

Marker 4: A Therapeutic Relationship

After you have successfully taken that first leap and shared your secret, consider making more of these jumps into deeper honesty. Deep honesty is not a way of life mastered the first time we try it. It is one of those very distant destinations. To move us closer to that way of life, we need markers that are in sight, like an ongoing and open relationship with the person we trusted with our secret.

There is a myth about therapeutic relationships and telling our secrets that we need to address. It is conventional wisdom that we get well only by "fixing" our problems; that we must somehow rectify what is wrong with us in order to find wholeness. We may then shrink from any therapeutic process because we feel that our secret isn't fixable. Yet the human psyche is not a machine that can be altered by mechanical steps.

Therapy and honesty are like quantum physics. Change can happen in our lives simply by observing our secrets: by paying attention to our dark thoughts and feelings rather than leaving them hidden. Our realities can be changed through nothing more than observation and awareness. We can find insight, strength, and new consciousness through the process of self-examination.

The goal is to develop a healthy and progressive relationship with a trained counselor who can serve as your guide through the dark woods. If you don't have good chemistry with the first, try another. If you are not making progress toward your goal of transparency with one, get another recommendation and take your work elsewhere.

The first three markers will take you far in the journey, but probably not far enough. The goal of sharing our secrets is to bring closure to them so they are stripped of their power to control us. Closure means ownership, acceptance, and even the embrace of our failures. Remember, we are moving in the direction of greater openness with other people and that journey is going to take you beyond your most trusted confidant.

Marker 5: Proportional and Thoughtful Honesty

Choose carefully the extent to which you divulge your secrets. Deep sharing is on a "need to know" basis. You will likely need to tell at least a few people what you have been hiding…for your own healing and for theirs. Your counselor can help you consider these additional steps toward wholeness because you want to be real with the right people, not the most people.

Thoughtful honesty might include, for instance, people who have been injured by your secret. You may need to make some kind of restitution for closure to take place. The Twelve Step Program gives wisdom here. One step says: *Make direct amends to such people wherever possible, except when to do so would injure them or others.* You can find freedom from your secrets without placing unjust burdens on another.

Often, the injury to others is the very act of keeping the secret from them. Perhaps you are dating someone but know the relationship is a dead-end for you. You have kept this unpleasant reality to yourself because you don't want to hurt them (self-deceptive rationale) or expose yourself to a negative reaction (closer to honesty). Eventually, you will need to be honest with this person who is also stuck with your secret.

Your aim is authentic and appropriate openness, which is not a matter of expressing everything that stirs your heart or pops into your head. You don't get extra credit for being a skeleton exhibitionist. You may want to write a "tell all" book one day, but otherwise, stay away from mindless openness.

Honesty is not always giving a critique of your sensitive other's apparel, even if they ask your opinion. You don't need to belittle the idiosyncrasies of your co-workers, even if they deserve it. You are under no obligation to share all of your opinions on politics, religion, or the weather.

The matters that require your transparency are the matters that actually define your relationships with yourself and others. This means openness varies based on the depth of those relationships. You don't need to tell your typical next-door neighbor you have a gambling problem, unless perhaps he presses you to handle his investments. If he asks you to drive him to the doctor but you're at the horse track, you don't owe him the full explanation. He's just a neighbor, not your spouse, best friend, or business partner.

There are also times when you should withhold information for the good of the other. This is discretion, not secret keeping. There is little value in dumping your toxic secrets on the most convenient person at hand. Don't drop off your skeleton with someone who doesn't have the capacity to deal with it.

Remember, the point of this book is to be free of a certain category of secrets: namely, those that interfere with and diminish our daily living and relationships, those that lead us into deeper duplicity, and those that create chronic fear or stress. These are the secrets that need to come out, and they need to come out fully and carefully. Listen to them closely and they will tell you where and when they need to be told.

In your journey toward freedom, aim at proportional honesty. Deeper relationships require greater honesty. Put them on a sliding scale together, weigh the importance of the relationship, and then give it the equivalent level of honesty. If you want a significant and mutually satisfying relationship, it will require real transparency.

Progress Indicators

We have been giving you reference points along the road to personal freedom and deep honesty with others. When we keep these markers in sight and move toward them, the road to personal awareness becomes clearer. Our journey so far has been outward. After this exercise, we will begin to identify markers for the inward journey to freedom.

Let's take a moment before we make that shift to consider our progress thus far. It would be nice if our minds had odometers to tell us how far we've come, or gauges that would report the status of our health, or pop-up boxes that informed us of updates to our operating progress. In reality, we'll have to settle for more subtle signs.

Moving into deeper honesty with yourself and others will cause some changes in your life that can be observed if you look closely. If you see any of the following, be encouraged that you are making progress on the journey.

1. **You are finding yourself less judgmental of other people**. This is not to say that you become blind to injustice, but you do find yourself less eager to celebrate or focus on what's wrong with other people.

2. **You feel less stressed by implicit and unspoken expectations**. That voice in your head that always whispers about failure and inadequacy will begin to fade as your unrealistic expectations about life lose their importance.

3. **You are speaking less about your own interests and achievements.** At work and in social settings you will not feel the same need to posture and prove. Instead, you will be freer to engage others about their own lives and struggles.

4. **You are becoming more vulnerable in relationships**. You will find yourself admitting that you made a mistake. You will openly apologize when you're wrong and try to make things right. You might even be honest about your weaknesses instead of trying to cover them.

5. **You are leaning into self-reflection**. After a conversation, you wonder what prompted you to embellish the story and you look more deeply than before. You feel tightness in your stomach and question what might be bothering you instead

of finding a distraction. You cry during a television movie and look for the inner emotional connection that is about you, not the movie plot.

The road toward freedom moves us to greater honesty with other people and the outward expressions of our lives. But the journey also takes us inward. We must turn and face what is deep inside our souls. When we open our closets and our lives to the light, we find more treasure than we imagined.

Marker 6: Your Secrets

Our secrets become our guides when we release them. It may sound strange but it's true. The road to freedom and transparency is one of progressive discovery. The concepts we share about our inner reality may not be familiar to you, so allow us some time to introduce them. These insights will serve as captivating reference points on your amazing journey.

The best teachers in life aren't tenured professors at Ivy League schools. They aren't the classic schoolmistresses of days past. Our best teachers have always been our most difficult struggles; our most painful experiences and our deepest sufferings; the realities we don't talk about. Yet we avoid these teachers like The Plague or early morning college classes.

Your secrets and the pain they have caused stand ready to be your best teachers and valuable markers. Obsessive habits or addictions, for instance, can teach us something about ourselves we wouldn't discover any other way. Almost every alcoholic in recovery will tell you this.

Maria's drinking problem began when she could not pass the bar exam. She was devastated that she had spent so much time and money on school and would not be able to reap the benefits. She became bitter, cynical, depressed, and self-destructive, especially when half her paycheck went to pay student loans.

It was not until years later, after her alcoholism had seriously impaired her life, that she discovered the real pain she was trying to mask. And the reason she discovered this buried secret was because she finally owned and "confessed" to the problem of her drinking.

It was at an AA meeting when it finally hit home. Maria was not just devastated that she couldn't be an attorney. She was devastated that she had disappointed her father, again, and would probably never get the blessing or approval from him she wanted so badly.

"I thought my problem was drinking," she said. "Then I thought it was my father and others who had not affirmed or supported me. Then the light came on and I knew the real problem was that I didn't accept or respect myself. I didn't believe in myself. I didn't embrace myself. My addiction was just a symptom of that."

Our failures, indiscretions, dark thoughts, and feelings are clues that point us toward the hard realities of life that need to be in the light. They hold keys to our fuller awareness and wholeness as human beings. So face them and move toward them. As you get closer, you'll begin to see what was hidden.

- You lie to impress others because your worst life experience as a child was one of rejection;
- You're getting emotionally involved with someone on Facebook because your marriage is just a shell and you can't face it;
- You secretly gamble for some excitement because you hate your job and it sucks the life out of you;
- You have a secret post office box because your father beat you when he found you hiding stuff in your room.

Follow the tracks of your secrets and they will take you to the truth. Even though the reality may be ugly, this truth is the path to new awareness. Name and get honest about your life experiences that lurk in the shadows. Hold the incongruent aspects of your life up to the light. Accept and embrace the reality that can now become your guide to freedom.

Don't run from your struggles. Dig into them and learn from them. *The only thing worse than suffering is wasted suffering. There is a priceless diamond to be found down in that pressure and pain.* That diamond is the real you, and when you practice radical honesty, this new reality begins to show itself. The real you is your ultimate reference point in your journey to honesty and freedom because it is created and connected to Ultimate Reality, or God.

Marker 7: The Truest Of Two

Find and follow your truest inner compass—a process that is complicated by competing identities. Our trials and tribulations have a way of revealing that we actually have two identities: one we know very well and another mostly beyond our awareness. The first is temporal, superficial, and a lousy guide. This recognized identity is the one we work so hard to dress up and protect by hiding our secrets. Sadly, it is also the "you" that cannot find a way to freedom or wholeness.

In this marker section we will describe both identities, but let's look first at the one we know so well: the one that leads us to dead ends.

The Deceptive You

The reason we end up with a closet full of secrets and a duplicitous life is that we have followed the least reliable internal compass we have. We have done this thinking it's the *only* internal compass we have. This transitory identity is the "you" that has been forming since conception; an identity shaped by DNA, early brain formation, and your varied life experiences. This is the "idealized you" designed to survive and thrive in our world. It is the "you" that seeks to be valued by others and wants a name for itself. But, it already has one.

It has been called the Ego and many other things. We like to call it the *Fictional Self* because it's never really at peace with reality. It is a necessary identity, but not our ultimate one.

Our culture values success in its various forms, so the Ego derives personal value from transactions, status, or achievements. The Ego is dependent upon the respect, honor, and dignity given by others. It must constantly measure up to be of value. Therefore, the Ego must hide faults and weaknesses knowing they create deficits and diminish our sense of worth. The Ego is necessary for life in a meritocracy, but tragically, even when it wins the rat race, it still feels like a rat.

The Ego is also the Grand Bargainer/Manipulator. Its chief aim is survival, so it will hide your skeletons and soothe your conscience by volunteering at the soup kitchen. This "you" is always going to focus on external problems and remedies to avoid internal realities. Buddhists call this life "emptiness" for good reason.

Your Ego will try to be a guide in your quest for life, but it is utterly deficient in this capacity. Following it will be the proverbial dog chasing his tail.

Your Truest Self

The other "you," the one lesser known, is the ultimate marker. Use it as your North Star. Various religious traditions and many in the field of psychology have described this identity. It has been called the *Soul* or "God in you." Others call it the *True Self*: a gift of divine creation and consciousness. It is the "you" that is moved by beauty, drawn to love, connected to the divine, and aware of transcendence. It is the self that knows how to live in light and freedom, so trust it to lead you there.

We believe, along with most spiritual guides throughout history, that the Soul is our true identity. It lies beneath and beyond all the successes and failures of the Ego. Our True Self is different from the Ego in that it is a birthright and inheritance, not an achievement. It is bestowed with supreme value from our Creator and this value can never be earned or lost. Our True Self can be disregarded or denied, but it longs to be discovered and embraced. It wants to come into the light along with our secrets.

We are being drawn toward this deeper identity all the time, though most of us are too busy and distracted to pay attention. Even so, there are times when we sense a deeper existence within, if only for a moment. It might be watching a film that tells a story of healing or reconciliation. It might be looking out the window of an airliner at 35,000 feet. It might be a strange sense of longing that comes as you remember a childhood friend.

There is a reason we are drawn to archetypal stories like *The Ugly Duckling* and *The Velveteen Rabbit*. These are universal myths about the discovery of our true selves. We are not the ugly secrets that assault our egos. We are not human playthings to be discarded. We possess the swan-like beauty of the divine and we are real because we are loved perfectly by God. When we read these stories, our souls tell us they are true.

Follow the path to your True Self. Keep moving your Ego out of the way and discover that "you" are a priceless creation of God. Reject the Ego's markers of success, perfection, admiration and self-protection because they are illusory. Follow instead the "you" that is made for love and complete in love.

Who and What We Trust

Ultimately, we must decide who and what we trust, or who and what is true. That is not an easy task because we can follow anything from a whim to a tradition. We call the True Self our ultimate marker because it is the place of deepest connection to God and therefore to love. Love, we believe, is worthy of our trust.

If you saw the film, *A Beautiful Mind*, you were initially caught up in the delusion of a schizophrenic genius named John Nash. For much of the movie, you could not distinguish the real and the unreal, as was the case in real life for John.

In a similar way, we are all caught up in our own delusions of the Ego. Success, wealth, status, power, and pleasure seem like the most genuine necessities of a really good life. We can live in this deception all of our lives.

Continually carried away by his fantasies, John Nash eventually found his way toward Reality and a Nobel Prize. You see, John's wife Alicia stayed with him through his great delusions. Even when he could not accept it, she tried to show him what was real and what was not. It was torturous for both of them, but John began to trust his wife more than he trusted his own sense of reality.

John was able to live into a new reality not by being cured; not by being rid of imaginary faces and voices; and not by some new wonder drug. He was able to live in a truer light by trusting his wife's love more than his imaginings. He just kept clinging to her love because it showed itself to be true.

You have to trust someone or something other than the compass of your Ego if you are going to make your way to freedom. There may be help in a support group, a religion, a vocation of service, or a therapist, but we would point you back to the Source that is love.

We encourage you to trust the love of the One who created you and who is as close to you as your own soul. Your True Self has and always will be home to The Divine. This is where you will find a love worthy of your trust.

When you aren't sure about living in the light, look for and follow this authentic and indwelling love. It will progressively reveal itself to you as you move toward transparency. Let this love, which needs no external validation, be your guide as you become truer in your relationships. Let this unconditional love, which holds the universe together, be the North Star that brings you home at last.

Stages Of A Truer Life

You'll find that this journey to freedom, this path toward home, unfolds in stages that sometimes require significant shifts that may feel like "starting over." Don't be discouraged by this. Each restart will begin closer to your goal of freedom. When you lose your way, go back and find previous markers to get back on course. The markers we've named can serve you for a lifetime.

The road to deep honesty and freedom is not a quick trip to Grandma's house. It is a life journey that takes place in phases, so be prepared to feel both progression and digression. We should, however, move through some identifiable stages along the way.

In their research about how travelers have found their way to freedom and wellbeing, Alejandro Jodorowsky and others have identified four stages of passage. Those who find full resolution in each stage move toward the light of new awareness and freedom.

1. **Grieve and Give Up**. You must identify and fully grieve what you did not receive as a child, and give up trying to gain this by using other people. Many of us did not receive love, acceptance, affirmation, security, encouragement, or dignity as children. Discover your loss. Grieve it and give it up. It's too late for Mommy and Daddy to give you these things, though not to late to have them.

2. **Accept What Comes To You**. Receive the gifts you did not receive as a child as they come to you from God and from life.

Grace abounds in the universe when we look and when our hearts are open.

3. **Give To Yourself.** As an adult, you can give to yourself what others did not give you as a child, including love, acceptance, affirmation, security, encouragement, respect, and dignity.

4. **Give To The World.** When you no longer need from your parents or others what you can receive otherwise, you are empowered to give these gifts to others without condition or expectation. This is the path of fullness and wellbeing.

Our skeletons are products of our desperate attempt to get what our inner child wants but cannot receive. As we give up our secrets, however, we can learn to give up the grief that created them and take these steps toward greater light in our lives.

Beyond The Satire

We know that people don't find freedom from secrets or discover their truer selves just by reading a book. Yet we do hope we have encouraged you to begin this journey to a truer life that becomes its own deepest reward.

We must wrap this up, however, and in so doing we come full circle back to The Code and its satirical message. We hope on the road to freedom, instead of *dressing for diversion*, that you own your failures and foibles as great teachers. Rather than *mimicking master charlatans* as models of successful duplicity, we hope you will learn from examples of rarified integrity. If you're going to *take the offensive*, we hope that means a commitment to keeping it 100% real. Don't *fear failure* of performance or measuring up to others, but instead discover the depth of your intrinsic value as a person, regardless of your accomplishments. As for *plausible deniability*, why would anyone try to live by some covert standard designed for clandestine government operations?

Mutual Trust, contrary to our satire, is worthy of risk, just like love. Rather than some *personal diversion* to get a rest from the ridiculous, why not practice genuine respite for your soul? We do encourage you to *get better*, not at hiding your secrets, but at finding the best way to bring them to light. *Come out with flare* if that's what it takes, but coming out with *care* will lead to a better and longer lasting outcome of integrity.

God bless you on the journey, and enjoy that extra closet space!

Bibliography

Brown, Brené. *Daring Greatly: How the Courage to Be Vulnerable Transforms the Way We Live, Love, Parent, and Lead.* New York: Avery Publishing, 2015.

Brown, Brené. *The Gifts of Imperfection: Let Go of Who You Think You're Supposed to Be and Embrace Who You Are.* Center City, MN: Hazelden Publishing, 2010.

Burton, Robert. *On Being Certain: Believing You Are Right Even When You're Not.* London: St. Martin's Press, 2008.

Chopra, Deepak. *The Book of Secrets: Unlocking the Hidden Dimensions of Your Life.* Easton, PA: Harmony, 2005.

Coyle, Daniel. *The Talent Code.* London: Arrow Books, 2009.

Eagleman, David. *The Brain: The Story of You.* New York: Pantheon Books, 2015.

Eagleman, David. *The Secret Lives of the Brain.* New York: Vintage Books, 2012.

Goleman, Daniel. *Emotional Intelligence: Why It Can Matter More Than IQ*. New York: Bantam Books, 2005.

Goleman, Daniel. *Social Intelligence: The New Science of Human Relationships*. New York: Bantam Books, 2007.

Imber-Black, Evan. *The Secret Life of Families: Making Decisions About Secrets: When Keeping Secrets Can Harm You, When Keeping Secrets Can Heal You-And How to Know the Difference*. New York: Bantam Books, 1999.

Katie, Byron. *I Need Your Love: Is That True?* New York: Harmony Books, 2005.

Katie, Byron. *Loving What Is: Four Questions That Can Change Your Life*. New York: Three Rivers Press, 2003.

Kelly, Anita E. *The Psychology of Secrets (The Springer Series in Social Clinical Psychology)*. New York: Springer, 2002.

LeDoux, Joseph. *The Emotional Brain*. New York: Simon and Schuster, 1996.

Leibovich, Mark. *This Town*. New York: Blue Rider Press, 2013.

Lewis, C.S. *Till We Have Faces: A Myth Retold*. San Diego: Harcourt Brace and Co., 1980.

Lewis, Thomas, Fari Amini, and Richard Lannon. *A General Theory of Love*. New York: Vintage Books, 2000.

Lucas, Marsha. *Rewire Your Brain For Love*. New York: Hay House, 2012.

Peck, M. Scott. *The Road Less Traveled and Beyond*. New York: Simon and Schuster, 1997.

Powell, John. *Why Am I Afraid To Tell You Whom I Am?* New York: Thomas More, 1995.

Rohr, Richard. *What the Mystics Know: Seven Pathways to Your Deeper Self*. New York: Crossroads Publishing, 2015.

Rohr, Richard. *Immortal Diamond: The Search for Our True Self*. San Francisco: Jossey-Bass, 2013.

Ronson, Jon. *So You've Been Publicly Shamed.* New York: Riverhead Books, 2015.

Sarno, John E. *Healing Back Pain: The Mind-Body Connection.* New York: Grand Central Publishing, 2010.

Sarno, John E. *The Divided Mind: The Epidemic of Mindbody Disorders.* New York: Harper Perennial, 2007.

Tancredi, Laurence. *Hardwired Behavior: What Neuroscience Reveals about Morality.* Cambridge: Cambridge University Press, 2010.

Taylor, Steve. *Out of the Darkness: From Turmoil To Transformation.* Carlsbad, CA: Hay House, 2011.

A free eBook edition
is available with the
purchase of this book.

To claim your free eBook edition:

1. Download the Shelfie app.
2. Write your name in upper case in the box.
3. Use the Shelfie app to submit a photo.
4. Download your eBook to any device.

Shelfie

A **free** eBook edition is available
with the purchase of this print book.

CLEARLY PRINT YOUR NAME ABOVE IN UPPER CASE

Instructions to claim your free eBook edition:
1. Download the Shelfie app for Android or iOS
2. Write your name in **UPPER CASE** above
3. Use the Shelfie app to submit a photo
4. Download your eBook to any device

Print & Digital Together Forever.

Snap a photo

Free eBook

Read anywhere

The Morgan James
Speakers Group

↗ www.TheMorganJamesSpeakersGroup.com

We connect Morgan James published
authors with live and online events
and audiences whom will benefit
from their expertise.

Morgan James makes all of our titles available
through the Library for All Charity Organizations.

www.LibraryForAll.org

CPSIA information can be obtained at www.ICGtesting.com
Printed in the USA
BVOW08*1450190916

462609BV00001B/1/P